A Colonel Destined to Lead

Aditya Bhushan

This is a work of biography. The events and the incidents mentioned in the book are true and real. However, some names and characteristics have been changed, some events have been compressed, and some dialogues have been recreated.

First Edition: November 2017
Printed in India

ISBN: 978-93-87269-27-9

Printed at Brandigo Private Limited, Navi Mumbai.

Cover Design: StoryMirror

STORYMIRROR
Stories that reflect you

Publisher: StoryMirror Infotech Pvt. Ltd.
7th Floor, El Tara Building, Behind Delphi Building,
Hiranandani Gardens, Powai, Mumbai,
Maharashtra - 400076, India.

Web: storymirror.com
Facebook: @storymirror
Instagram: @storymirror
Twitter: @story_mirror
Contact Us: marketing@storymirror.com

Acknowledgement

Whenever I used to see the first page of a book with dedications to one's father, mother or wife, I wondered if this is some kind of a norm that authors have to follow. But, now having written a book myself, I can vouch for the feeling of the authors while acknowledging the role played by family members. All my family members were equally supportive of this project and I thank them from the core of my heart. However, the three people who bore with me over the last few months and believed in me were my mother Nita Prasad, my father Suniti Bhushan Prasad and my wife Akanksha Srivastav.

It was my father who told me throughout this journey that unless you try, you would never know if you would succeed or fail, and that kept me going. He is also responsible for introducing me to Vijay Nayudu, Col. CK Nayudu's grandson. For my mother, I would only say that she used to give me ideas whenever I faced any obstacle in this journey. And being the person I am, I would reject most of her ideas at first, only to agree to them later. In order to write a book, I wanted peace of mind and my wife ensured that there was no hindrance to this. She would never disturb me while I was writing and she also took up the additional responsibility of almost single-handedly running the house smoothly. Since, I was writing along with a full-time job, it meant that I was busy or travelling on most of the weekends. And my wife would get bored while being at home alone, but never did she show it. In addition to providing the moral support, she has done the first-round of editing of this book. Being my wife, she could bluntly tell me if a section sounded boring. My mama, Dr Lala Abhi Nandan also helped in proof reading few sections of the book and I thank him for that. Since he is a scientist, he would get into his reasoning mode and question me for any sentence written.

Apart from family members, my friends also encouraged me a lot. In fact, the seeds of the idea to write a book were sown in to my mind by my school friend Apurva Sharma. About a year ago, he had told me that I should give a shot at writing a book.

It has indeed been my good fortune that whomsoever I met for this book, was more than helpful to me. I think this was because of two things; first, they all have high regard for Col. CK Nayudu and second, because they all are good human beings. I can't thank Vijay Nayudu uncle (Col. CK Nayudu's grandson) enough, who is the sole reason for making this book a reality. I also owe a lot to former Indian cricketer Madhav Apte, who was always there whenever I needed a help.

Despite their old age, Vasant Raiji, the late MK Shukla, Rameshwar Pratap Singh and Waman Jagtap entertained me and answered all my questions patiently. I am grateful to them for this. I thank Sanjay Jagdale, Akshay Dhakad, Shrikant Rangnekar (son of former test player Khandu Rangnekar) and Professor Suryaprakash Chaturvedi for giving me some rare insights about Col.CK Nayudu.

I express my gratitude to the heroes of yesteryears – Chandu Borde, Salim Durani and Nari Contractor. I am also thankful to few more family members of Col. CK Nayudu - Pratap Nayudu (Col. CK Nayudu's grandson and son of Prakash Nayudu), Leela Vidyasagar (Col. CK Nayudu's daughter), Sangeeta Kanjnani (Leela's daughter), Manjula Rao (Vijay Nayudu's sister).

I am obliged by the support provided by journalist and writer, Clayton Murzello. He also provided me some rare scorecards from the Clayton Murzello Collection. I thank Mohandas Menon for allowing me to use statistics which cannot be found easily today. I thank Sanjay Jayawant who helped me in contacting many cricketers.

I am extremely grateful to the Madhya Pradesh Cricket Association (MPCA), Cricket Club of India (CCI) and Bombay Gymkhana for providing me with photographs of Col. CK Nayudu. I thank my publisher Story Mirror for giving me a chance to become an author.

Aditya Bhushan

Contents

Preface

A Colonel Destined to Lead is the fascinating story of Indian cricket's first superstar - Col. CK Nayudu. CK, as he was popularly known, started playing cricket at a time when the game was still in its nascent stages in the country. In fact, it was his innings of 153 runs for the Hindus against the visiting Marylebone Cricket Club (MCC) at the Bombay Gymkhana which paved way for India's elevation to test status.

Thus, it was only fitting that he went on to become India's first test captain in 1932. But he could well have not become the captain, had it not been for the generosity of the original skipper of the team - Maharaja of Porbandar. As luck would have had it, CK became the captain, but unfortunately his test career was short-lived. It is also sad that he could never be part of a winning test team. Test cricket came very late in his life and his prime days were with the Hindus team in the Bombay Quadrangular tournament in the 1920s and 1930s. He emerged as the highest run-getter in the tournament's history of two decades. Post retirement from test cricket, he remarkably led the Holkar team to four Ranji Trophy titles. CK's association with the Holkar team started in 1924 when Maharaja Tukojirao Holkar III had invited him to Indore.

For the Holkar team, he was a fatherly figure and no one dared to question him. The Holkar players admired him and followed all his orders obediently. One of his weirdest methods was to not allow the Holkar players to drink water on the cricket field as he thought it wasn't good for their fitness. CK was a fitness freak to say the least and this helped him to play the game for a long time. His first-class cricket career spanned over an astonishing 47 years.

He played his last first-class match at the age of 68 years.

Throughout his career, he was known for his aggressive and uncompromising style of captaincy.

Later on, when he became the Chairman of the national selection committee, he didn't change his approach. With CK, uncertainty was the only certainty. As a selector, he could jump into the nets and test out the fast bowlers himself or roll over few balls to the batsmen. In certain matters, he was very headstrong and it was due to his this behaviour that the great Vinoo Mankad was initially left out of the Indian team's tour to England in 1952. At home too, CK was a strict guardian, but loving nevertheless. He instilled the importance of hard work to his children and today they feel it an honour to have been associated with him.

Regrettably, the last session of his life turned out to be miserable for him. His opponents got together in a bid to humiliate him and started ignoring him. CK wasn't prepared for this and it was very painful for his fans.

Now that, it has been 50 years since he left for heavenly abode, one wonders about his relevance in today's times. Given his attacking style of batting and captaincy, it excites me to think how successful he would have been in today's era. Although, I feel it is unfair to speculate on such things, but in CK's case one can safely bet on his success even in the shorter formats of the game prevalent today. Also, I can confidently say that even today his style of play and methodologies seem pertinent. His story is an inspiration for anyone aspiring to take sports as a career.

Innings that put India on the World Cricket map

Once upon a time in colonial India, a 31-year-old Indian batsman was up against a touring cricket team from the Marylebone Cricket Club (MCC) at the historic Bombay Gymkhana. The very third ball which he faced was hit for a six. And for the next couple of hours, he dismissed the opposition bowlers by his mere presence. The manner in which he did bat was a sight to behold. 91 years have passed since then and most of the people who had watched that epic knock have left for heavenly abode. But just as the cricket writer Sir Neville Cardus has rightly said, "We remember not the scores and the results in after years; it is the men who remain in our minds, in our imagination." So, a certain Col. CK Nayudu's name comes to our mind whenever we think about the origin of Indian cricket.

Now, cricket is considered to be a team sport; but its history is full of scintillating individual performances. Be it a great batting performance or a great spell of bowling, individuals have often turned the outcome of umpteen matches. Even then, rarely has one single knock deemed to be significant enough to define the cricketing future of a nation. But Col. CK Nayudu's innings of 153 runs against the visiting MCC on December 1st at the Bombay Gymkhana in the winter of 1926 was one such innings which laid the foundation stones for Indian cricket.

To understand the significance of that famous innings by CK (as he was fondly called), we need to rewind the clock to an era when cricket was still taking its first step in the country. Although cricket had been introduced to the Indians by the European merchant sailors in the 18th century, India was far from being called a cricketing nation. India had not yet been awarded a test status and the game of cricket was not as popular in the country as it is today. There were only a handful of cricket clubs in some of the major cities. The game was played only in big cities those days and in fact, was regarded as the game of the Maharajas. Thus, it was considered very difficult for a commoner to take up the game of cricket. The only tournaments of repute played in the country were the Bombay Triangular and Quadrangular tournaments.

The tour of 1926-27 by the MCC was in itself significant as this was the first time that an official team from England was visiting India. After playing matches at Karachi, Rawalpindi, Lahore and Ajmer; the visitors had arrived in Bombay (now Mumbai). Their first match at Bombay was against the Hindus, who were the reigning champions of the Bombay Quadrangular. The Hindus had many big names of those days in their ranks like DB Deodhar, LP Jai, P Vithal and Col. CK Nayudu among others. Despite this, even the staunchest supporter of Indian cricket was not expecting the Hindus to challenge the hegemony of the Englishmen.

The MCC team led by Arthur Gilligan had so far been unbeaten in the series and the result at Bombay was expected to be no different. The visitors batted first and scored 363 runs, courtesy a century by Guy Earle. Earle scored 130 runs with the help of 8 sixes in just about 90 minutes. The Bombay crowd, who had never seen such a kind of hitting before, was thrilled, to say the least. But they did not have the faintest idea about what was in store for them on the next day. They were going to witness one of their own stars bat better than Earle.

In reply to the MCC innings, the home side began cautiously and ended day one with the score at 16 runs for the loss of one wicket. When play resumed on the next day, Hindus lost their second wicket at the score of 67 runs. And in walked the ever-elegant CK. Old timers say that there was a unique style in CK's walk to the pitch which could be matched by none. What followed for the next two hours or so took not only Indian cricket but the entire cricketing world by storm.

CK took guard and made his intentions clear from the outset.

It started raining sixes and boundaries from the bat of CK. On a number of occasions, he hit two consecutive sixes. In one of medium pacer R Wyatt's overs he hit 22 runs. Now, CK was known for hitting long sixes and aggressive batting in the Quadrangular matches. But to do it against a MCC side which had many first-class and test cricketers was not an easy task. Describing CK's sixes, Australian writer Edward W Docker wrote, "Crack another six, this time to the right of the pavilion and not only the ground burst into tremendous sustained roar, but even the umpires were seen to clap vigorously." It is said that one of CK's sixes landed on the Gymkhana roof and the second landed on the tennis courts behind after clearing the pavilion. Now, anyone who has been to Bombay Gymkhana may argue that the ground is not a big one as compared to many other grounds of the world. But even then, the audacity of his hitting had left everyone spellbound. Also, during those days, it wasn't a common sight to see batsmen hitting the ball in the air. To constantly hit in the air that too with a bat which weighed only a fraction of the bats used today, did require some special talent.

Slowly, the news about CK's whirlwind batting started spreading around and spectators began to storm the Bombay Gymkhana. It is indeed fascinating to believe that in an age when there were no television sets or mobile phones, the word about CK's innings reached different parts of city almost at the speed of his cracking shots. Amongst many of CK's admirers was Bombay's eminent Jurist MC Chagla. He had reportedly left court proceedings midway to get a firsthand glimpse of the fireworks at the Bombay Gymkhana. And by the time CK resumed his innings post lunch, each available vantage point had been occupied by fans like Chagla. CK eventually hit 13 fours and 11 sixes in a score of 153 runs in about two hours' time before getting out to the bowling of medium pacer George Geary.

Remembering that Homeric innings, former first-class cricketer and cricket historian Vasant Raiji who had also witnessed CK bat that day says, "Back then, I was too small to understand the finer points of the game. All I remember is that there was a huge crowd. People were shouting about sixes and CK did hit a lot of sixes." Raiji is 97 years old now and is probably one of the few people alive to have witnessed the mayhem live at Bombay Gymkhana. But his eyes lit up as he started speaking about the innings. This speaks volumes about the knock and probably CK himself. Raiji goes on to say, "He (CK) was an artist. He put India on the world cricket map with that innings."

Another young boy who was among the crowd at Bombay Gymkhana on that day was famous cricketer Vijay Merchant. Merchant was just 15 years old then and years later he described it as one of the best innings he had seen. In one of the articles, Merchant had, later, written that after the end of day one, he had told his mother that Guy Earle's quality of batting was much better than he could have ever imagined. But CK's innings on the next day made Merchant set new benchmark of what to expect from a batsman.

CK's hit of 11 sixes in that innings was then a record in First-Class cricket. During his innings, CK had got able support from LP Jai who had scored 53 runs and SR Godambe who scored 58 valuable runs. The Hindus ended their innings just seven runs short of the total made by the MCC. In their second innings, MCC scored 74 runs for the loss of one wicket and the match ended in a draw. Despite the draw, the Indians had made a statement with CK's knock. For people who talk about psychological victory in test matches, this was an apt example of such a win. Such was the impact of CK's sixes that the next day a cartoon had appeared in a local newspaper showing a group of spectators pleading on the sill of the University clock tower (which was near the Gymkhana): "Don't hit us CK, we are not playing!"

In recognition of this innings, the MCC had presented a silver bat to CK. Today, the bat rightfully resides in the premises of the Cricket Club of India (CCI), Mumbai, an institution which had a special place in CK's heart. The bat was presented to the CCI by one of CK's daughters - Chandra Nayudu. While presenting the bat to the CCI, Chandra Nayudu had said, "I decided to present it to the CCI museum because it would be the biggest tribute to my father who is held in high esteem. The bat was a true recognition of his splendid knock and I wanted to perpetuate his memory."

With that single knock CK had announced the arrival of Indian cricket to the cricket fraternity. It was a trailer of things to expect from Indian cricket in future. His innings was screaming at the ears of the Imperial Cricket Conference (as the International Cricket Council was called in those days) officials that India was ready to make an entry in the world of cricket. His innings also came up for a lot of praise from the English media. And for an Indian to get applauds from the English press in the colonial days was nothing short of a miraculous achievement. For the first time in history, the Englishmen were forced to stand up and take notice of an Indian cricketer's performance.

It did bring about a paradigm shift in the way Indian cricket was perceived by the Englishmen. In fact, couple of years after this match, the MCC skipper Gilligan himself lobbied for India's elevation to Test status. Due to the efforts of Gilligan and several others, the Indian cricket board was formed in 1928 and India eventually played their first test match in 1932. But it was CK's swashbuckling innings on that eventful day at the Bombay Gymkhana which had carved a small place for India on the world cricket map.

That innings by CK has been engraved in the history of Indian cricket forever. It laid the base on which the tower of Indian cricket stands tall today. And as cricket statistician Anandji Dossa had said that it changed Indian cricket. Probably for the first time, Indian cricket was being viewed with a sense of respect and CK was the prime reason behind this new status.

The Silver bat presented to CK by the MCC in recognition of his innings of 153 runs which resides in the CCI today

Cricket Club of India (CCI), Mumbai

CK's Scrapbook presented to the CCI by Chandra Nayudu

Hindus & Bombay Cricket

Cottari Kanakaiya Nayudu was born in Nagpur and spent the early part of his life in the orange capital of India. Since the beginning, young Kanakaiya preferred to stay outdoors and would become restless if kept indoors. Although he indulged in many games like boxing, running, hockey, high jump and wrestling among others; he had taken a special liking for cricket from an early age. Giving an account of CK's early interest in the game of cricket in her book A Daughter Remembers, Chandra Nayudu writes, "He had taken to playing cricket when he was about six-seven years old. His love of the game stemmed from the fact that his uncle and father had spent their varsity years in England in an atmosphere reeling with cricket." So, from an early age itself CK spent most of his time playing cricket. As his grandson, Vijay Nayudu, who also represented Madhya Pradesh in Ranji Trophy, spoke about his grandfather's love for the game, he said, "CK just lived for cricket. Yet to see anyone as dedicated to cricket. Cricket was his religion."

Coming back to CK's childhood, it did not take long before CK was inducted in the school cricket team. He made quite a name for himself in the locally well-known Beadon Shield tournament. So, while it was clear to everyone around him that Kanakaiya had exceptional cricketing skills, but what he needed was proper guidance. Often, we have seen that young talent goes waste in the absence of proper grooming. For a sportsman, this guidance in the initial days more often than not comes from one's family. A conducive atmosphere at home coupled with supportive parents can do wonders to raw talent. While there have been exceptions to this rule and people have excelled at sports despite family problems, but no one can deny the positive impact that family support plays in building the career of a sportsperson. Thankfully, young Kanakaiya got all the backing at home and this played a big role in shaping his career. This also displays the importance that the Nayudus gave to sports, as during those days rarely did parents think of sports as a career for their wards.

His father Cottari Suryaprakashrao took special interest in Kanakaiya's game and acknowledging his father's role in his upbringing in cricket he had said; "My cricket coach was my father to whom I owe a good deal of my success in later years." There is an interesting story from CK's younger days about the part played by his father in shaping his cricket career. The world of cricket regards CK as an aggressive batsman, but that wasn't the case always and had it not been for his father's intervention he could have well remained a defensive batsman. It so happened that the great KS Ranjitsinhji was Suryaprakashrao's friend and when he saw young CK bat, he said to Suryaprakashrao, "Why doesn't he hit the ball?" This comment coming from a man who had played test cricket for England had to be taken seriously and Suryaprakashrao did just that. Suryaprakashrao told CK, "If you want to play cricket, you will have to learn to hit every bowler on every pitch. Go out into the rain and sun and make yourself hardy". And hence, the famous aggression of Col. CK Nayudu was born. His father also instilled a sense of fearlessness in him while facing fast bowlers. Suryaprakashrao described a fast ball to young CK as one which beats the batsman, the wicket-keeper and reaches the boundary with the speed of thought. He further went on to tell CK that one shouldn't flinch while playing fast bowling, but should instead hit it. So, the famed fearlessness of CK can also be attributed to his father.

With such guidance, CK's crescendo in cricket continued through school and college tournaments. But the arena that Nagpur had to offer was not enough to satiate young CK's talent. He needed a bigger stage to display his repertoire and Bombay provided him with the same. The city of Bombay which was given as a dowry in the marriage between King Charles II and Portuguese Catherine of Braganza to the East India Company in 1661, had become the cricketing hub of India by the 20th century. The Hornby Vellard project is credited with uniting the seven islands of Bombay. Similarly, the Presidency, Triangular, Quadrangular and Pentangular matches can be said to be the Hornby Vellard project for cricket in the City of dreams. The tournament began as Presidency matches between the European and the Parsis in 1892. With the addition of the Hindus in 1907, it assumed the title of the Triangulars. When a team representing the Muslims joined the tournament in 1912, the name changed to the Quadrangulars and it finally became the Pentangular with the introduction of the fifth team comprising of the remaining communities called as the 'Rest'.

Since its inception, Bombay Presidency matches drew immense attention of the people. People who could not get inside the ground, followed the matches from the vantage point of trees or through small holes in the tents. These matches were played by the best talent from across the country. It is said that these matches implanted the seeds for the future of Indian cricket. The matches were played in a carnival atmosphere and played a crucial rule in the evolution of cricket in India. About these tournaments, Vasant Raiji had rightly said that no future historian of Indian cricket can ignore the important role it played in the development of cricket in the country.

Hence, coming to play in Bombay was a significant step in CK's career. Now, he would be up against the very best not only in the country, but will also get a chance to play against the Europeans, some of whom were seasoned county cricketers. CK made his debut in Bombay cricket in the Quadrangular tournament in 1916 at the age of 21 years. This happened when he was invited to play for the Hindus against the Europeans. It should be noted that this was CK's first big match against a quality opposition. In this match, CK came in to bat at number 9 and scored 27 runs. The highlight of his innings was the six with which he had opened his account. And with this six, CK's fruitful association with the Hindus began. An association which brought the best out of him and this period can arguably be considered as his prime. His first scoring shot in the Quadrangular was a sign of the things to follow from his bat. Describing CK's six hitting prowess, Vasant Raiji writes in his book Story of the Bombay Tournament, "In later years, the crowd expected sixes from him every time he came out to bat." Now we don't know the exact number of sixes that he hit throughout his career due to the absence of detailed statistics of many matches, but we do know for sure that he hit quite a many of them.

During that time, the Hindus had a formidable lineup comprising of the Palwanker brothers (P. Baloo, P Shivram, P Vithal & P Ganpat), DB Deodhar, Dr. HD Kanga and LP Jai among others. The Hindus won the tournament for the first time in 1919-20 and CK played a key role in the victory. In the first match against the Parsees, CK made scores of 49 not out and 56 in the two innings, helping his team win the match by six wickets. Even in the finals against the Muslims, he made a valuable contribution of 45 runs and gave good support to P. Vithal who had scored a century. The Hindus eventually won the match by an innings and six runs.

In the next year's finals against the Parsees, CK hit his first century of the Quadrangular scoring 121 runs. However, the Parsees escaped with a draw and the tournament of 1920-21 had no title winners. CK continued his good form in the subsequent editions of the Quadrangular. When the Hindus won the title for the second time in 1923-24, CK played a pivotal role throughout the tournament. In the finals against the Europeans, he scored half-centuries in both the innings thus helping the Hindus win the match by 9 wickets.

CK's batting talent often overshadowed his bowling skills. As a result, till now the Bombay and Poona (few editions of the tournament were held in the Deccan Gymkhana in Poona) crowd had only seen CK wield his magic with the bat. But CK as a cricketer had much more to offer. CK bowled right-arm off-breaks and was often used as a partnership breaker. He showed his caliber with the ball in the 1924-25 edition, returning with figures of 3-28 against the Europeans. In the same match, he had scored 135 runs in the first innings. In the first innings of the finals against the Muslims, he was the lone batsman to get a half-century for the Hindus. Although the Hindus lost the finals, yet again CK had left his imprint on the tournament.

The Hindus continued their domination of the Quadrangular tournament by winning the title in successive years in 1925-26 and 1926-27. The finals of the 1926-27 edition was one of the most closely contested games in the history of the tournament. In a low scoring match, the Hindus defeated the Europeans by a slender margin of 11 runs. With a score of 31 runs, CK was the second highest run getter in the second innings behind DB Deodhar who had scored 49 runs. CK's good performances with both bat and ball continued over the subsequent editions of the tournament.

In due course of time, CK took over the reins of captaincy from P Vithal. An interesting event took place under his captaincy in the 1935 finals against the Muslims. The Hindus needed 366 runs to win and they were also losing wickets very quickly. CK's brother CS Nayudu had taken 9 wickets in the match and was resting in the hotel as he was down with fever. Seeing the quick fall of wickets, CK summoned him to come to the Bombay Gymkhana to bat as the last man. However, by the time, CS arrived at the ground, the match was declared completed. The Hindus were bowled out for 145 runs and the scorecard recorded CS as absent.

By 1935, despite being 40 years old; CK had clearly emerged as the most popular player of undivided India. His popularity can be gauged from an incident when a satirical pamphlet was released by a section of the committee members to protest the decision of not making him the captain of the Hindus. The story goes that certain committee members of Hindu Gymkhana did not want to have him as captain for reasons best known to them and so instead of him Yuvraj of Patiala was appointed as the captain. The remaining members who wanted CK to continue as the skipper came up with an innovative idea to mock the committee and released a pamphlet inviting applications for the post of captain of the Hindu Gymkhana. The pamphlet called only the Maharajas & Yuvrajs to apply for the post. Also, it mentioned that they shouldn't know anything about Quadrangular Cricket. Anyone who possessed skill, seniority and long experience were also debarred from applying as per the pamphlet. In a clear target at the selection committee, it further said that the appointment would be done on a probationary basis of one innings and a new captain may be selected for the second innings of the match. This pamphlet was distributed on the ground and the Yuvraj was booed by the crowd when he took the field.

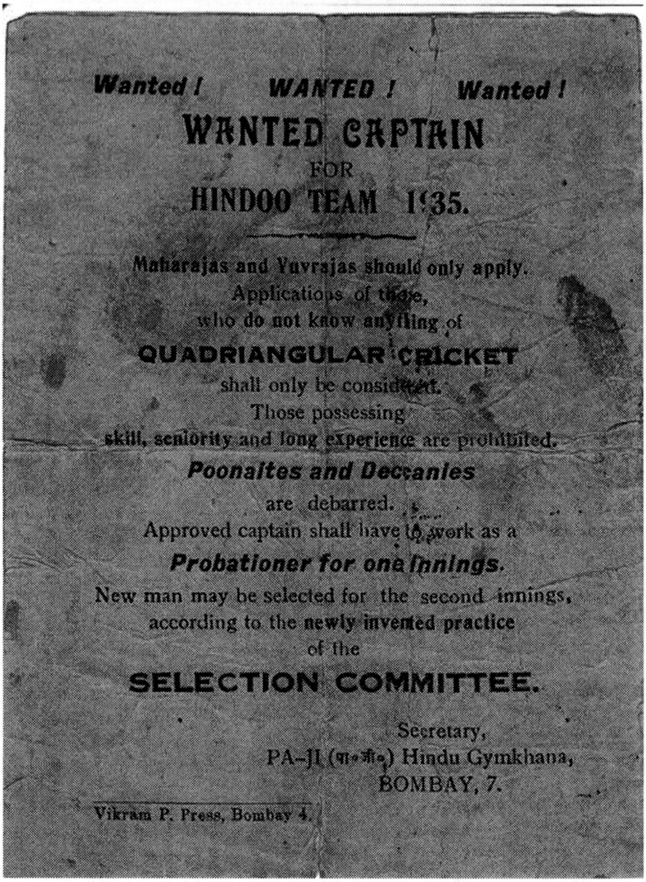

Wanted ! WANTED ! Wanted !

WANTED CAPTAIN

FOR

HINDOO TEAM 1935.

Maharajas and Yuvrajas should only apply.
Applications of those,
who do not know anything of
QUADRIANGULAR CRICKET
shall only be considered.
Those possessing
skill, seniority and long experience are prohibited.
Poonaites and Deccanies
are debarred.
Approved captain shall have to work as a
Probationer for one Innings.
New man may be selected for the second innings,
according to the newly invented practice
of the
SELECTION COMMITTEE.

Secretary,
PA-JI (पा॰जी॰) Hindu Gymkhana,
BOMBAY, 7.

Vikram P. Press, Bombay 4.

The Pamphlet released by few committee members to protest the decision of not making CK the captain of the Hindus

On another occasion, a friendly match featuring him drew more crowd than a regular match between the Hindus and the Muslims. It so happened that CK was dropped from the team by the Hindu Gymkhana Committee members for a match against the Muslims in CCI. Certain other gymkhana members were against this decision and as a mark of protest they organized a friendly match at the Hindu Gymkhana on the same day featuring CK. Such was CK's aura and popularity that when the crowd at CCI came to know that their beloved CK was playing at the Hindu Gymkhana, they all rushed over to the Hindu Gymkhana. The crowd adored

CK and he rarely disappointed them. At times, he used to play in matches at two different venues on the same day. Confirming this, Vijay Nayudu recalls that Capt. Mushtaq Ali had told him that once after CK's innings got over in CCI; he came over to the Hindu Gymkhana to take part in the match being played there.

With CK in their ranks, the Hindus enjoyed tremendous success in the Quadrangular tournament. Overall, they won the title six times, the last being in 1936-37 which was also the last year of the Quadrangular. It goes without saying that CK had emerged as a clear hero of the Quadrangular matches. With 1934 runs in 25 matches at an average of 48.35, he was the highest run-getter across two decades of the Quadrangular tournament. He scored five centuries across different editions which is also a record for the Quadrangular. On the field as well, CK took 27 catches and made it to the list of top three fielders. Speaking about CK's performance in Bombay cricket, noted writer Prof. Suryaprakash Chaturvedi says, "When there was no test cricket, CK Nayudu dominated the Quadrangular and Pentangular cricket in Bombay. He was considered as the most popular and valuable batsman of the tournament."

CK continued to thrill the crowd with his performances in the Pentangular tournament. However, slowly with passage of time it was felt that this format of tournament which had teams based on religion was creating disharmony amongst the communities. Renowned radio commentator and sports journalist AFS Talyarkhan had led the movement to abolish the Pentangular tournament. In a newspaper article, he had written, "Is there no enjoyment, no sport, no life worth living, except when the words Hindu, Muslim and Parsee come into play? Are Indians born into this world to believe that nothing, no sport, can be enjoyed unless it is communal". Even the Father of the Nation, Mahatma Gandhi had opposed the Pentangulars as he was against communalism in any walk of life. But if we are to believe the cricketers who played in these tournaments, they never felt the communal divide. CK himself had once said that instead of creating divide, the Pentangular had brought communities together. Other great cricketers like Vijay Merchant, Vijay Hazare and Capt. Mushtaq Ali also concurred with CK's view. In fact, commenting on this issue writer Edward Docker had said; "If ever India is to win communal unity it will be on the cricket fields, and cricket fields of Bombay in particular."

Now, people may have different opinions on the role that Bombay cricket played in bringing communal unity. But one thing which cannot be questioned is the positive impact that Bombay cricket had on the career of CK and Indian cricket in general. And like always, the City of dreams had lived up to its expectation. It helped a certain Cottari Kanakaiya Nayudu realize his cricketing dream.

Bombay Gymkhana Today - The place where CK played in his prime

Bombay Gymkhana Today - The place where CK played in his prime

CK arrives in Indore

Around the same time that CK was making rapid strides in Bombay cricket, the cricketing scene in Indore was also gaining momentum. And the man behind this cricketing revolution in the city was the then ruler of Indore, His Highness Maharaja Tukojirao Holkar, the III. Now, Indore in the early part of the 20th century was the headquarters of the British Central Agency. But, like most of the Indian cities of that time it did not have any major following for cricket. Maharaja Tukojirao wanted to change that. He was a great cricket lover who left no stone unturned in ensuring a bright future for Indore cricket. In 1913 he built a cricket ground in the city and this meant that young Indorians now did not have to go far from their homes to play the gentleman's game.

Slowly, the game of cricket started gaining prominence under the Holkar dynasty and the next major milestone in the history of Indore cricket came in 1916 with the foundation of the Yashwant Cricket Club. This club gave a platform for budding cricketers to showcase their talent. From 1917 onwards, all the major colleges in Indore had their own cricket teams and the locals had many cricket teams to choose their loyalty from. Teams like the Yashwant Cricket Club, Daly College and the Holkar College became particularly popular among the locals. Maharaja Tukojirao's seriousness about spreading the game of cricket in Indore can be gauged from the fact that he had arranged for specialists from abroad to impart cricket coaching to his son Yashwant Rao. This coaching was also extended to the friends of Yashwant Rao. But despite this enthusiasm by Maharaja Tukojirao, if Indore wanted a successful cricket team of its own then it needed cricketers of repute who could compete at the national level. During those days, it was a common practice for

Maharaja Tukojirao Holkar

Maharaja Yashwantrao Holkar

Maharajas to get the best available players from across the country for their teams. And in 1924, Maharaja Tukojirao just followed this norm by beginning a hunt for players from outside Indore to form his own cricket team.

By 1924, word about CK's exploits had spread to different parts of the country. Being a keen cricket follower, Maharaja Tukojirao had also heard about CK's extraordinary skills. He invited CK to Indore and the rest as they say is history. With this single move, the Maharaja changed the cricketing landscape of Indore forever. Although CK accepted the offer; it is worthwhile to note that the decision to move to Indore may not have been an easy one for CK. He had a vast ancestral property in Nagpur and to leave everything to move to a different city was easier said than done. The death of CK's father at roughly the same time could also have played a role in him accepting Maharaja's offer. As Chandra Nayudu writes in her book, "With the death of his father hanging heavily on his mind and heart, CK accepted the offer and came over to Indore leaving Nagpur the place of his birth for good." Thus, CK came to Indore; incidentally the land where his father had served as the Chief Justice of the Holkar state way back in 1905. CK was made a captain in the Holkar army, but his primary task was to build a cricket team for the Holkars.

The Maharaja knew that in order to truly produce a

competitive team, he needed few more players to support CK. So, along with CK, Maharaja Tukojirao also brought in cricketers like SM Joshi and Janardan Navle to Indore. They were also offered jobs in the Holkar army, but like CK their foremost work was to play cricket and win matches for the Holkar cricket team. The Maharaja was not just after building a cricket team for the Holkars, he was fostering a cricketing culture in Indore. He ensured that his players received ample support in their pursuit for cricketing excellence. There was never a compromise in cricketing matters during his reign. He never shied away from spending that extra rupee to get the best of equipment for his team. He provided his players with the best in class cricket gear and clothing. It is said that each player of the Yashwant Cricket Club had a Guns & Moore cricket bat. Also, their dresses used to get stitched by famous tailors in Bombay like Esquith & Lord's or Rankins of Calcutta (now Kolkata). Given the economic conditions of an average Indian in those days, one can conclude that these things would have additionally contributed in enticing the Indorians towards cricket and eventually making the Holkars a champion cricket team.

By the time, Maharaja Tukojirao passed on the throne to his son Yashwant Rao in February 1926, cricket had already come a long way in Indore. But still the seeds of cricket sown in by Maharaja Tukojirao needed to be nurtured. And in this regard, Maharaja Yashwant Rao followed in the footsteps of his father. He ensured that there was no change in the cricketing policy of the Holkars. Under him, Indore cricket and CK in particular flourished. CK and Maharaja Yashwant Rao became good friends over time and CK also served as his Aide-de-Camp (ADC). Later, Yashwant Rao conferred the honour of a Colonel to CK in the Holkar army. Commenting on their relationship with Maharaja Yashwant Rao and the royal family, CK's daughter Leela Vidyasagar, who currently stays in Canada said; "Our relation with Maharaja Yashwant Rao was very close because of cricket. Nana (as CK's children called him) would go to the palace every day when not playing. As kids, we would go to the palace when invited to play with the Holkar princess Usha Raj. Our mother would be usually invited for religious functions. The Maharaja himself would come home too, sometimes without notice, late at night, driving his Rolls Royce. Nana and Maharaja would chat for hours on cricket and other topics."

And it was not just the Maharaja; but Her Highness Maharani Margaret Lawlie Holkar, second wife of Maharaja Yashwant Rao was also fond of CK and his family. It is said that she was the person behind the allotment of a bigger house to CK. It so happened that CK had fallen ill and the Maharani had come to their house to see him. While leaving, her car got stuck at the gate of CK's 'Kila House' (it was in front of the fort, and thus it was called the Kila house). This prompted the Maharani to wonder how could someone (leave alone CK) live in such a small house. Hence, CK was immediately allotted a palatial house called the 'Suraj Kothi' which suited his status. Later on, 'Suraj Kothi' became synonymous with Holkar cricket and the Holkar players considered it as their second home.

Today 'Suraj Kothi' or the Holkar team may not exist, but the legend of Col. CK Nayudu has stayed on. The city of Indore considers CK as it's own son. Many people in this most populous town of Madhya Pradesh may not even know that their favorite cricket hero originally hailed from Andhra Pradesh. The fact that the city remembers him even 50 years since his death is a manifestation of the love and respect that the people have for him. And I confirm CK's popularity with my rickshaw driver. His response to my question of whether he knows who Col. CK Nayudu is, *"Arre haan, unka to ek bada statue hai na Nehru stadium ke bahar"* (Oh yes, there is a big statue of him outside the Nehru stadium). Nehru stadium doesn't host international cricket matches any longer, so the statue of a cricketer outside the stadium might come as a surprise to many. But for the city of Indore, Col. CK Nayudu was much more than a mere cricketer. He gave a sporting identity to the city. If Maharaja Tukojirao was the person who showed the cricketing light to Indore, then CK carried on the torch to greater heights. Pratap Nayudu, who is one of CK's grandsons, and is also an international arm-wrestler, aptly summarized the connection between CK and Indore when he said, "From what I have heard, it won't be wrong to say that CK brought Indore on the world cricket map."

India makes its debut at Lord's

While CK was marching ahead as a cricketer, the honour of representing one's nation in a test match was missing from his otherwise illustrious resume. He had not played a test match as India had not yet acquired a test status. But this was about to change soon.

As mentioned earlier, the late 1920s saw a growth in the stature of Indian cricket. Efforts were in full swing to make India a part of the elite test playing nations. One meeting which is of significance in this regard is the one in February 1927 at the Roshanara Club in Delhi between MCC skipper Arthur Gilligan, Grant Govan, Anthony De Mello and the Maharaja of Patiala - Bhupinder Singh. It was in this meeting at the Roshanara Club that the idea of a cricket board for India was floated.

Apart from Arthur Gilligan, the other three were not cricketers of any repute, but one thing which was common among them was the passion for cricket. Grant Govan was a Delhi-based British industrialist and an avid sports enthusiast. De Mello worked with Grant Govan and Maharaja Bhupinder Singh was a keen cricket follower himself. The Maharaja also owned the highest cricket ground during those days in Chail (a hill station in Himachal Pradesh). The decision to form the Board of Control for Cricket in India (BCCI) was taken around 9 months later at the same place by representatives of various provinces and princely states. And eventually, the BCCI was formally formed in December 1928 with Grant Govan as its president and De Mello as its secretary. The two represented India in the Imperial Cricket Conference in May, 1929. Along with Maharaja of Patiala, the two were instrumental in getting a test status for India.

With this newly acquired test status, a tour by the All-India Test cricket team to England, the home of cricket, was scheduled in 1932 featuring one test match and few first-class games. So, the next task at hand was to select a formidable Indian team for the tour. Dr. HD Kanga, AL Hosie and Ahsan-ul-Huq were entrusted with this all-important task initially. But Dr. HD Kanga & AL Hosie declined this job. They were then replaced by KS Ghanshamsinhji of Linmbdi and Maharaja Kumar of Vizianagram. Maharaja of Patiala and KS Duleepsinhji were the co-opted members of the selection committee. Elaborate selection trials were held at Patiala and Lahore where top 57 players from the country were invited. 52 of those invited, attended the trials and finally 18 privileged players made it to the squad for the historic tour. Even though the team was being called as an All-India test team, such was the influence of the royalty that it was still deemed necessary for it to be led by a Maharaja. Hence, despite having some very good cricketers, Maharaja of Patiala was chosen as the skipper. But he had to withdraw due to illness and the baton of captaincy then fell on the shoulders of Maharaja of Porbandar - Natwarsinhji Bhavsinhji. So, the All-India Test cricket team led by Maharaja of Porbandar set out for their first ever test tour to the land of cricket's originators. Now it is a different matter that the captain of the All-India Test cricket team hardly had any first-class experience. He was the captain only due to his royal lineage.

Before the first test match, the Indian team played ten three-day matches and were victorious in four of them. CK was the star performer in these matches leading up to the first test match, scoring 764 runs. Amongst his many noteworthy performances was the century which he scored against the MCC at the iconic Lord's ground. He had a near ideal debut at the mecca of cricket, scoring an unbeaten 118 runs and taking four wickets.

The Indian team defeated Worcestershire just before the first test match and hence were in the right frame of mind before the D-day. At least that's how it seemed to an outsider, but something else was brewing up in the team. Despite being the captain, Maharaja of Porbandar knew his own cricketing limitations very well. In a great gesture, which was unheard of from the Maharajas, on the eve of the test he told the team that CK Nayudu would lead the team instead of him at Lord's. However, the players were not ready to be led by a commoner. They were fine if a Maharaja who did not have the desired cricket skills led them, but it was unacceptable for them to be led by a common man. This was the unfortunate mindset of few of the Indian players of those days. As a result, Maharaja of Porbandar was woken up in the night by many players who told them that they would not play under CK. In a desperate attempt to redeem the situation, the Maharaja of Porbandar sent a cable to Maharaja of Patiala in India. Patiala immediately replied, ordering them to play under CK. The players were now left with no option, but to have CK lead them. Thus, CK Nayudu became India's first test cricket captain. Now, although the captaincy of the Indian team came accidentally to CK, there was never any doubt about his leadership skills.

And one needs to give credit to the Maharaja of Porbandar for the fact that he relinquished the captaincy in favour of the more able CK Nayudu. In fact, he had kept himself out of many first-class matches on the entire tour to give a chance to more deserving cricketers. As Vasant Raiji said to me, "Maharaja of Porbandar was a sensible man. He kept himself out and gave the captaincy to CK."

So, after much of preparation, drama and fanfare the day that every Indian cricket fan had been waiting for had arrived. On a sunny day on June 25th, 1932, India made its test debut at Lord's and became the sixth test playing nation after England, Australia, South Africa, New Zealand and West Indies. The day of June 25th is an auspicious day as far as Indian cricket is concerned. 51 years since making its test debut, the Indian team won their first One Day International (ODI) World Cup on the 25th day of June in 1983 at the same ground.

Coming back to India's first test match, it was a three-day test match as during those days, this is what was offered to the new entrants of test cricket. Bombay-born English skipper Douglas Jardine won the toss and decided to bat first. It is an irony that the same Douglas Jardine was at a time suggested as the man to captain India by Anthony De Mello. The Indians made a dream start picking three English wickets in the first hour and conceded only 19 runs. Pacer Mohammad Nissar wreaked havoc in the English top-order. But the home side was not going to succumb so easily against the newbie of cricket. Jardine led the English fightback with an innings of 79 runs, helping his team reach a respectable total of 259 runs. He was well assisted by wicket-keeper Les Ames who scored 65 runs. Nissar became the first Indian to take a five-wicket haul in an innings and finished with figures of 5 for 93. Skipper CK Nayudu also chipped in with two wickets, one of them being that of his counterpart - Jardine. In response, the Indians made a cautious start and ended day one with 30 runs for no loss. On Day two, Indian top order offered some resistance to the English attack and it looked as though India could give a real fight to their experienced opponents. But after CK who top-scored with 40 runs got out, the innings crumbled. They lost the last six wickets for 50 runs and were bowled out for 189 runs. It must be noted that during this innings, CK battled physical pain and batted with an injured hand. In their second innings, the English top ordered faltered yet again. For the second time in the match, they were saved by their skipper Jardine who scored an unbeaten 85 runs. He stitched together a partnership of 89 runs with left-hander Eddie Paynter who was the second highest scorer of the innings with 54 runs. England declared their innings at 275 runs for the loss of 8 wickets, thus setting the Indians a target of 346 runs. Jahangir Khan with figures of 4 for 60 was India's most successful bowler in the second innings. India's second innings was a repetition of their first innings. Yet another batting failure by the top and the middle-order left them reeling at 108 runs for the loss of seven wickets. Only a late flourish by Amar Singh who scored 51 runs was the saving grace in the entire innings and helped them get to a total of 187 runs.

Thus, India had lost their first test match by a huge margin of 158 runs. But the Indians had not faired as badly as the score line suggested, considering it was their first test match. As the 'Manchester Guardian' wrote, "The result of the match suggests an easy victory. As a fact, England suffered moments of severe stress. They had to go through an amount of labor and anxiety not at all represented in the score sheet's statistics". Well, the scorecard suggests that the loss was due to a batting failure. But what it does not tell is that the Indians had been handicapped by injuries to CK, Nazir Ali and Phiroze Palia. Commending the performance of the Indian team, the 'Morning Post' wrote, "England vs All India was one of the most interesting matches seen at Lord's for a long time. Had it not been for casualties, the visitors might have made a very near thing of it." 'Morning Post' even went on to lament that fact there was no second test match on offer for the Indians on that tour.

Recalling that match, CK wrote in his diary, "I am satisfied that we played aggressive cricket. Although, we were defeated, but we were not humiliated. I am hopeful that history will remember this match with pride and people will realise that we had given our everything. We had gone with the aim of winning and while playing at Lord's we did not think about any other result".

The Indian team played few more first-class matches after the test and CK emerged as the team's most successful batsman of the tour. There is a fascinating tale about how one of his hits against Warwickshire at Edgbaston had landed in another county. Apparently, CK hit a huge six of Jarett which cleared the ground and passed over River Rea, which acts as a natural boundary between Warwickshire and Worcestershire. The distance of the hit could have been anywhere between 110 to 115 meters. This is comparable with the long sixes hit in today's era of T20. And if we bring into picture the bats used in those days, respect for that shot and CK goes up by many notches.

CK finished the tour scoring 1,618 runs at an average of 40.45. He also had a good outing with the ball taking 65 wickets at an average of 25.53. The other top performers of the tour were opening bowlers Amar Singh and Mohammad Nissar. Owing to CK's performance in England, he became the first Indian to be selected in Wisden's cricketer of the year in 1933. Wisden wrote, "Tall and well-proportioned, Nayudu is eminently fitted by nature to be a good cricketer and his doings for the Indian team fully bore out the good accounts of him that had come to us by reason of his excellent performances in his own land. Above all else, he was a very strong player in front of the wicket, his driving both to the off and on being an outstanding feature of his batting. For a first-class man he had one little peculiarity in that he conveyed the impression of being rather late in making up his mind to drive. This, however, did not detract in any way from his skill or effectiveness. Possessed of supple and powerful wrists and a very good eye, he hit the ball tremendously hard but, unlike the modern Australian batsmen, he lifted it a fair amount." Wisden also admired him for leading the team in difficult circumstances. CK's grandson Vijay Nayudu also tells me that his grandfather was a great strategist. In fact, he attributes some credit to CK's strategy in Nissar's five-wicket haul in the first test match at Lord's.

Next year, the English team came for a full tour to India to play three test matches. The first test match was held at Bombay Gymkhana, the place where CK had plundered Arthur Gilligan's MCC team seven years earlier. This time around, CK played more sedate knocks of 28 and 67 runs in the two innings. In the first innings, most of the Indian batsmen got a start, but failed to convert it into a big score. As a result, the Indian innings ended at 219 runs. In reply, the Englishmen took a big lead and scored 438 runs, courtesy a century by Bryan Valentine and half-century by skipper Jardine. In the bowling department for the Indians, Mohammad Nissar again returned with a five-wicket haul. The second innings brought in a better performance by the Indian batsman. Debutant Lala Amarnath & CK put together 186 runs for the third wicket. Lala Amarnath went on to score a century, thus becoming the first Indian test centurion. But the batting collapsed again after the fall of Amarnath & CK. The entire team was bowled out for 258 runs, giving a target of only 40 runs to the visitors. India lost the match by 9 wickets.

In the second test match played at Calcutta, Indians were able to draw the match despite following on in the first innings. This time, the bowler in CK had come to the fore, picking up three wickets in England's first innings. India lost the third test match at Madras by a huge margin of 202 runs. The only talking point for the Indians in this match was fast-bowler Amar Singh's seven-wicket haul. But despite these losses, Indian cricket under the able leadership of CK was moving ahead. Impressed by the progress made by Indian cricket, Jardine had said that one day India will be challenging other countries on equal terms. Sadly, he did not live enough to see his words come true. Today, the Indian team is one of the top teams in cricket across all formats.

It was unfortunate that when the Indian cricket team toured England next in 1936, CK was removed from captaincy for non-cricketing reasons. Yet again, a Maharaja was made the captain. This time, the man in-charge of the team was Maharaja of Vizianagram and Vizzy (as he was called) was not as generous as Maharaja of Porbandar had been during the last tour. Despite an attempt by other cricketers asking him to quit captaincy in favour of CK, he declined and is said to have even got angry at the proposal. Former Indian cricketer, Madhav Apte also tells me that Vizzy should have never become the captain and CK was the one who deserved to lead India on that tour. To give you an idea about Vizzy's cricket competence (or lack of it), he had once failed to even get selected for the Hindus. Apart from not being given the captaincy, CK was at the receiving end of Vizzy's wrath on the tour. Vizzy had reportedly asked Baqa Jilani to insult CK and also rewarded Jilani with a test cap in return. Not surprisingly, Jilani went on to play only one test match for India. If all this was not enough, then in one of the most shameful incidents in Indian cricket history, Lala Amarnath was sent back home before the first test on disciplinary grounds. He had been targeted on the tour by Vizzy, who had not allowed him to take rest despite knowing that he was carrying an injury. In one of the matches at Lord's he was asked to pad up, but deliberately not sent out to bat. He got his turn only few minutes before the close of play and as a result of it he was very angry. So, when he came back to the dressing room, he said, "I know what is transpiring". This was more than what Vizzy could tolerate and with the support of few players, he demanded an action. Unfortunately, for the Indian team, the man who was the leading all-rounder on that tour had to go back due to the whims and fancies of Vizzy. In another display of weird behavior fostering division in the team, Vizzy had reportedly offered Capt. Mushtaq Ali a gold watch to run out Vijay Merchant. Thankfully, Mushtaq declined the offer.

Not surprisingly, the score line at the end of the series read as 2-0 in England's favour. It could well have been a complete whitewash had it not been for centuries by Indian openers Vijay Merchant and Capt. Mushtaq Ali in the second test match at Manchester. In the third and which was going to be India's last test match for the next decade, CK scored a fighting knock of 81 runs. This was CK's highest score in test cricket, but it was not enough to avoid an innings loss for the visitors. Sadly, this match turned out to be the last time that CK was seen adorning the Indian cap on a cricket field. Overall, CK's own performance on the tour was much below expectation. Although, he scored over 1000 runs and took

51 wickets in first-class matches, he appeared to be a pale shadow of the man who had excelled on the previous tour in 1932.

By the time India resumed playing test cricket in 1946 post the second world war, CK was already 51 years of age and had retired from international cricket. Thus, the test career of India's first captain was short-lived to say the least and it spanned over only seven test matches. But is it fair to judge CK's caliber by only his test numbers of 350 runs at an average of 25 runs per innings and 9 wickets at an average above 40? I begin to wonder whether CK would have been as famous as he is now if he had not become India's first test captain. Vasant Raiji solves this dilemma for me. Even at his age, Raiji angrily responds to me by saying, "Why shouldn't CK be famous? He certainly would have been famous. He had all-round skills, as a batsman, as a captain and as a fielder". He goes on to add that test career came late in CK's life. His best years were probably the mid-1920s.

In today's age when numbers and records have become the hallmark to judge the greatness of a cricketer, I believe it might not be easy for our generation to understand the phenomenon named CK. As Capt. Mushtaq Ali had once said, "CK cannot be weighed against record books nor do centuries form a yardstick of his greatness. The present generation of cricketers cannot imagine the type of cricket he played".

The glorious Holkar era

While CK had retired from test cricket, he continued playing domestic cricket. And the laudable part about his cricket was that there was no drop in the intensity of his game even while playing domestic cricket. He approached domestic cricket with the same level of dedication as he had approached test cricket. In hindsight, this could have been one of the major reasons for his success in Ranji cricket post hanging up his boots from test cricket. He made his Ranji Trophy debut playing for the Central India team when the Ranji Trophy was launched as "The Cricket Championship of India" in 1934. For the next few years he represented Central India with a fair amount of personal success. But he was destined to be associated with the Holkar cricket team again and this time for unmatched success.

Given Maharaja Yashwant Rao Holkar's love for the game, it was only a matter of time before he got a team of his own participating in the Ranji Trophy. His dream came true in 1941 with the establishment of the Holkar Cricket Association and the Holkars made their Ranji debut in the same year under the captaincy of CK. For the next decade or so, CK transformed the Holkars into a champion side. Between 1944 to 1954, the Holkars won the Ranji Trophy four times and finished as runners-up on six occasions. Now, such a consistent run is a remarkable achievement for any team under any circumstances. But if we take into consideration the fact that the Holkars had joined the championship only few years back, the enormity of this performance goes up by leaps and bounds.

And this golden run was primarily a result of the fruitful

partnership between Maharaja Yashwant Rao Holkar and CK. Maharaja Yashwant Rao provided the vital support off the field and CK left no stones unturned on the cricket field. Former Holkar player Rameshwar Pratap Singh reaffirms this statement and says, "CK had made the Holkar team and Maharaja Yashwant Rao Holkar gave him a free hand in cricketing matters". Maharaja Yashwant Rao trusted CK and it is said that under his rule, CK's words were the final authority as far as cricket was concerned. This was a stark departure from many of the other Maharajas who interfered in the cricketing affairs of their states despite having little or no knowledge of the game. He wasn't the usual whimsical royal, at least for the game of cricket. And the beneficiary of this prudent behavior of Maharaja Yashwant Rao was Holkar cricket.

Now, although CK had the support of the Maharaja and a freedom to run the Holkar cricket in the manner he wanted to, but as they say, 'With freedom comes great responsibility'. And CK had the responsibility of building a bright cricketing future for the Holkar team. CK instilled a sense of discipline in the Holkar team and people say that CK's strictness played a major role in making the Holkars Ranji champions. A typical day for the Holkar team would start with few rounds of the ground followed by around two hours of net practice. Former Holkar player Waman Jagtap recollects that CK was very punctual and he expected the same from his players. During the match, the players were expected to stay in the tent as CK believed that one could learn a lot by watching the game live. The Holkars were known for their aggressive style of cricket, as this was the brand of cricket which CK endorsed.

In addition to being the captain, he was the de facto coach and selector for the Holkar team. CK handpicked players who he felt could help him take the Holkars to the pinnacle of domestic cricket. He got in players like Capt. Mushtaq Ali, MM Jagdale, JN Bhaya, BB Nimbalkar and Khandu Rangnekar among others who became the backbone of the Holkar team. For a brief period of time he had also roped in the great English cricketer Denis Compton who was then posted at Mhow (a cantonment in Indore district).

Given his stature in Indian cricket at that time, most of the Holkar players were in awe of CK and used to address him as 'Sir' or 'Colonel Saab'. He was the commander in chief who had a firm belief in what he did. The only person who could probably stand up to him was Khandu Rangnekar. Khandu could ask questions to CK and he would patiently listen. But then, as Madhav Apte told me that this was mainly because of Khandu's personality and the fact that CK was himself fond of Khandu. Khandu was the perfect lieutenant on whom Colonel Saab relied upon a lot. On one occasion, few days before a Ranji match in Indore, CK was informed that Khandu could not take part in the match as he was in Calcutta. CK immediately sent a message, asking him to come by rail, road or air. As luck would have had it, no tickets were available in train or flight and Khandu had to come back by car. Khandu finally reached on the morning of the match after travelling for two nights and a day. Seeing Khandu's condition, CK said, "OK you will bat at number seven. Go and have some sleep". So, there was some respite for Khandu, but it was short-lived. Soon wickets started falling and CK said, "Khandu ko uthao" (wake up Khandu). Khandu went out to bat in the center at the fall of the next week. He did not disappoint CK's belief in him by scoring a century. Khandu also respected CK a lot and he had once said to his son that if he had to choose between paying to watch Colonel Saab & Sir Don Bradman, he would probably pay to just watch Colonel Saab walk. Former Indian star Salim Durani also vouches for CK's walk, he says, "Even if CK scored 10 runs, people were happy just to see him walk. He had a graceful walk". Unfortunately, we don't have any recording of that majestic walk which Khandu preferred to watch over the batting of a gentleman with a test average of 99.94.

Yet another stalwart in the Holkar team whom CK had a great faith in was Capt. Mushtaq Ali. Mushtaq was also CK's discovery when he had observed a 13 years old Mushtaq play in Indore. Impressed by the young boy, CK had taken special interest in his development as a cricketer. Mushtaq's batting flourished under CK's guidance in the Holkar team. During one of the matches, the Holkar team needed around 100 runs to win and Mushtaq Ali was batting. A well-wisher came to CK and said, "Colonel Saab,

Mushtaq ko bolo thoda dhire khele" (Colonel Sir, ask Mushtaq to play a bit slowly). To this CK replied, "No no, let him play as he wants. He will play well". So, it can be said that when CK had confidence in a player, he would allow him to play as he wanted without much interference.

Till now, we have only associated worlds like strict and disciplinarian with CK. While, there is no denial about this, but the person CK was not all about just being strict and stern. Vijay Nayudu considers his grandfather as a person who though was firm, but was generous at heart and gave an opportunity to many cricketers. CK did expect his players to give cent percent, but at the same time he would be there for the players whenever they needed any help. And this help was not restricted to just cricketing matters. He often also provided financial help for the Holkar players. Vijay Nayudu recalls the days in Indore when people would come to CK for help and he would just tell Vijay, "Amma se packet lekar ago" (Get the packet from grandmother). This packet usually contained some money and was given to those seeking financial aid from CK. This was a routine affair at CK's house and more often than not, he provided the desired help.

Talking about CK's personality, Khandu Rangnekar's wife Vimala Tai Rangnekar said, "First impression of CK was that he was very upright and stern looking. But he had a softer side to him as well". When CK had first met Vimala Tai at the Yashwant club, he had asked her about what she did in her spare time. Then he even arranged for tennis lessons for her. Later on he made her the manager of the Holkar team and always stood by the decisions made by her. Empowering a lady during that era was rare and in that sense CK probably was visionary. Another occasion when the lighter side of CK came out was when he was watching Denis Compton (who was also an accomplished footballer for Arsenal) practice football. Compton scored a goal through a banana kick and CK commented, "Good fluke Dennis". Not pleased at the remark, Dennis replied that he could hit such a goal on seven out of ten occasions and he went on to prove CK that his goal was not a fluke.

With this combination of toughness, and care when needed,

he was a fatherly figure for the Holkar team. Like any loving father who would want the best from his child while maintaining a tight rope on them, CK ensured that his team remained disciplined. He rarely did praise his players on their face. At the most he would say, "well played" or "well bowled". But both CK and Maharaja Yashwant Rao would stand by the team whenever they wanted a help or had a reasonable request. Rameshwar Pratap Singh recounts an incident from the semi-final of 1945-46 Ranji Trophy between Holkar & Mysore team at Indore which goes on to show the same. When Rameshwar came out to bat in the match, the Holkars were already in a very strong position with the score at 706-6. Five of the Holkar batsmen - KV Bhandarkar, Chandu Sarwate, MM Jagdale, CK & BB Nimbalkar had already scored a century in the innings so far. Rameshwar also started scoring runs and was on 80 runs when Maharaja Yashwant Rao who was present at the ground asked CK to consider declaring the innings as the team total had already gone past 800 runs. This score was thought to be sufficient for a big victory. RN Zutshi who was a member of the selection committee and later on went on to become the principal of the Daly College (the college in which Rameshwar studied) had overheard this conversation. He requested the Maharaja to allow the innings to continue for some more time so that his school's ward Rameshwar could also get a century. Rameshwar says, "The Maharaja agreed to the request." Thus, Rameshwar scored a century and Holkar declared their innings with the score at 912-8, which was a record then for the highest total in Ranji Trophy. Rameshwar's century was the sixth of the innings, which is still a world record for the maximum centuries in a single innings in first class cricket. But this would not have been possible had the Maharaja or CK not given a go-ahead for the continuation of the innings. Sarwate ripped through the Mysore batsmen in the first innings, picking 9 wickets. Holkars went on to win the match by a margin of an innings and 213 runs. They continued their good form and also won the final against Baroda, courtesy performances by the Nayudu brothers CK & CS. While CK scored a double hundred in the first innings, CS took 5-wickets in both the innings.

This was the first of the four Ranji trophy championships won by the Holkar team. Their second and third Ranji trophy titles came in 1947-48 and 1950-51 respectively. In the 1947-48 finals, they defeated Bombay by 9 wickets. Though CK did not score much, he was in action with the ball taking five wickets in the match. Captain Mushtaq Ali and Chandu Sarwate were stars of the 1950-51 finals against Gujarat. While Mushtaq scored 187 runs in the first innings, Sarwate scored a double century in the second innings. The Holkars won the match by 189 runs.

1952-53 was the last time that the Holkars were crowned as Ranji champions. Their finals against Bengal at Eden Gardens that year was one of the most entertaining Ranji finals ever played and it also displayed CK's confidence in his team. Batting first, Bengal team had scored 479 runs. In reply, the Holkars took a slender lead of 17 runs which in the end proved decisive in their victory. The star of the Holkar innings was BB Nimbalkar who scored 219 runs. Having conceded a first innings lead, the Bengal team knew that their only chance of getting a hand at the Ranji Trophy was to go for an outright victory. They declared their innings after scoring 320 runs for the loss of five wickets in less than 50 overs. This meant that the Holkars were set a target of 304 runs in the fourth innings. In such circumstances, most of the captains would have adopted the safer approach to save wickets and get a victory on the basis of first innings lead. But as Prof Suryaprakash Chaturvedi says, "CK was made of some different soil". He instructed his batsmen to go for the target. In the process the Holkars lost wickets at regular interval and when the 9th wicket fell, there was still an hour and a half left in the game. The two Holkar batsmen at the crease were Hiralal Gaikwad & SD Dhanwade. They somehow managed to survive the end overs and gave a perfect farewell to their skipper CK. Their final score was 177 runs for the loss of 9 wickets. Captain Mushtaq Ali was the top scorer with 46 runs, followed by CK with 25 runs. Maharaja Yashwant Rao, who was present at the Eden Gardens threw a lavish party at the Grand Hotel to celebrate his team's victory.

After leading the Holkars to their fourth Ranji trophy victory, CK announced his retirement from first-class cricket. Although he came back from retirement in 1956-57, it was not for the Holkars and instead he turned up for Uttar Pradesh. By this time the Holkar team itself had been dissolved and was replaced by a Madhya Bharat team. This team later on became part of the Madhya Pradesh team as the Indian states were reorganized.

Today, the city of Indore is home to the Madhya Pradesh cricket team and their home ground is appropriately named as the Holkar stadium. It shares some part of the land with the erstwhile stadium which had witnessed the Holkars being crowned Ranji champions on three occasions. And the people behind this new Holkar stadium have ensured that every corner of the stadium echoes with the memories of the glorious Holkar era. The reception area is filled with photos of the victorious Holkar team. Former cricketer and selector Sanjay Jagdale passionately told me that they have ensured that there is an appropriate mix of the Indian and Holkar great's while naming the different stands of the stadium. While one gallery contains stands named after former greats of Indian cricket like Vijay Hazare, Ajit Wadekar, Sunil Gavaskar, Kapil Dev, Sachin Tendulkar and Anil Kumble, the other gallery has stands named after the Holkar greats from the bygone era like JN Bhaya, MM Jagdale, Khandu Rangnekar, Hiralal Gaekwad, Chandu Sarwate and CS Nayudu. The two pavilions are named after the two most famous cricketers from the Holkar team Col. CK Nayudu and Capt. Mushtaq Ali. Then there is a room which has on display the belongings of CK. There is his trunk when he was the A.D.C to the Maharaja and also his dress. These priceless artefacts were shown on television when the Holkar stadium had hosted its first test match in 2016 between India and New Zealand.

With these kind efforts, the officials of the Madhya Pradesh Cricket Association (MPCA) have kept the legend of the glorious era of Holkar cricket alive. It is an irony that despite having some very good cricketers in their ranks, the Madhya Pradesh team has never been able to create the same magic which existed in the Holkar days under CK. This compels us to think whether the Holkar team would have become the champion side that it became sans CK. Nevertheless, the Holkar team gave the perfect opportunity to CK to prove his leadership skills and he did come out with flying colors.

Victorious Holkar team with their maiden Ranji Trophy title in 1945-46

Holkar team with the Maharaja & Maharani

Victorious Holkar team with the Ranji Trophy title in 1951-52

Holkar team with their last Ranji Trophy title in 1952-53

Illustrious wall at the Holkar Stadium with photos of the winning Holkar teams

Holkar Stadium Today

CS Nayudu Stand

Col. CK Nayudu Pavilion at the Holkar Stadium in Indore

Col. CK Nayudu Pavilion at the Holkar Stadium in Indore

Capt. Mushtaq Ali Pavilion at the Holkar Stadium in Indore

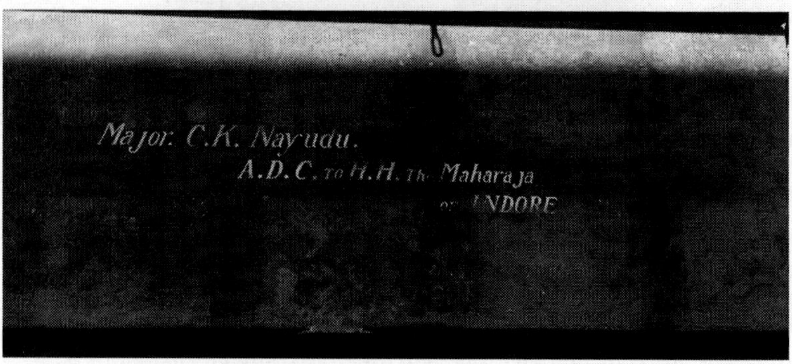

Belongings of CK in display at the Holkar Stadium

Belongings of CK in display at the Holkar Stadium

Six centurions from the Holkar team in the 1945-46 Ranji semi-finals against Mysore. Standing: (From left to right): Rameshwar Pratap Singh, MM Jagdale, Col. CK Nayudu, BB Nimbalkar. Sitting: KV Bhandarkar, Chandu Sarwate

Dare not question The Colonel

So, what was the secret behind Colonel Saab's success as a captain of the Holkar team? Was it because the team had exceptional players or was it because of his inspiring captaincy? Which cliché would be appropriate to describe CK & the Holkar team - A team is only as good as the captain or A captain is only as good as the team? The fact is that the Holkar team did have some great players (many handpicked by CK himself) and CK's visionary captaincy gave them the right direction. And a combination of these two aspects took the team to greater heights.

So, it might be difficult to come up with one single reason for Colonel Saab's success with the Holkar team. But what came out clearly from my meeting with several cricketers who either played under him or saw him captain was that he was a very aggressive and assertive captain. Defensive tactics had no place in his captaincy. He would lay out a plan and direct his team to play as per that.

Credit should also be given to the players of the Holkar team who were a dedicated lot and went about to obey their master's order. While CK adopted many unmatched ways to prepare the Holkar team for tough battles, but the weirdest of his methods was to not allow the Holkar players to drink water on the field as he felt that it was not good for fitness. The Holkar players rarely dared to go against this diktat of Colonel Saab. Referring to CK, his former Holkar teammate Rameshwar Pratap Singh said, "Unke saamne kisi ki awaaz nahin nikalti thi" (No one could speak in front of him). Another Holkar player Waman Jagtap also confirms this and says, "Kisi ki himmat nahin hoti thi beech mein paani maangne ki" (No one dared to ask for water in the middle). He could get angry if anyone asked him to compromise this rule, like he had got during the 1952-53 Ranji Trophy semi-finals against Maharashtra at Indore. It was pretty hot in Indore and during the toss Maharashtra skipper Madhusudan Rege had asked CK, if they could have water breaks after every 45 minutes. CK gave him an eggy look and said, "If you want you can drink, my boys will not drink".

Even though, during those days most of the matches were not played in the summer season, it would have been a herculean task for the players to be without water on the field. So, whether they liked it or not, the Holkar players had no option, but to be without water on the field. On this, Chandra Nayudu has written an interesting story in her book narrated to her by Khandu Rangnekar. Apparently, once during a drinks interval a thirsty Chandu Sarwate quietly drank water and thought that he had escaped CK's eyes. When CK did not immediately reprimand Sarwate, everyone thought that Sarwate had narrowly escaped from the ever-watchful eyes of CK. But much to Sarwate's dismay, CK had seen this act of defiance. The consequence was that he dropped Sarwate from the team for the next match. No one other than Khandu had the guts to question CK, so he went and asked the reason for it. CK's response was one word - "indiscipline". No amount of cajoling could get Sarwate back in the team for that match. Khandu even approached Maharaja Yashwant Rao asking him to intervene, but the Maharaja refused to interfere. The Maharaja told Khandu that CK was the supreme authority as far as Holkar cricket was concerned. He had supposedly said, "Look I may be the ruler of the state, but CK is the ruler of the game. I will not interfere in his management of the affairs of cricket". In my interaction with former Holkar players or others who had played against CK, it came out distinctly that there was no compromise as far as the 'no water' rule was concerned. The only exception to this rule of not having water on the field was made for Englishman Denis Compton, when he turned out for the Holkars. Now, the true value of this directive of not having water on the field can be debated. But, his grandson Vijay Nayudu feels that there certainly was merit in this practice; although he too realized it very late.

This kind of strictness might seem uncalled for to most of the people. But then, the results that he achieved with his unyielding approach is extraordinary. The other question which comes to one's mind is whether the players were happy under him. In my opinion the Holkar team would have been a contented bunch despite the regulations imposed by CK. I say this on the basis of my interaction with former Holkar players and also because I don't think an unhappy team can be as successful as the Holkar's were under CK. So, to an outsider it would seem as though the unsaid rule in the Holkar team was - Don't mix with the Colonel. But the reality is as far from truth as possible. Yes, there is no doubt that CK had his own ideas which may not have been acceptable to everyone. But they regarded him as the patriarch of the Holkar cricket family and knew that he always had the best interest of the team in mind.

The players feared him, but at the same time respected him a lot. Waman Jagtap said that he considers himself fortunate to have played alongside CK. He also learnt a lot about discipline from CK. As per him, CK taught the Holkar team to respect the game of cricket. It is said that no one could disrespect the cricketing equipment in front of him. On his part, CK was always there to guide youngsters and the doors of his house 'Suraj Kothi' were always open for the Holkar players. His daughter Leela Vidyasagar told me that if the players visiting Indore needed an accommodation, they would stay in CK's house for months (sometimes years) together. He considered the entire Holkar team as his family and the team also often used to party at his house. Rameshwar Pratap Singh reminisces that CK used to ask him to get his projector to 'Suraj Kothi' so that everyone could watch a movie. CK was also a great connoisseur of music. In fact, whenever he visited Calcutta, the great singer Kundan Lal Saigal would come to meet him and sing the whole evening for him.

So, in principle, CK wasn't against the enjoyment of his players. But at the same time, he could get angry when any player showed signs of indiscipline. In such cases, he wouldn't leave the player alone after reprimanding him, but would help him to get back on the right track. Like, once he was furious at Waman Jagtap when the latter was suspended for passing some remarks after drinking. Disciplinary actions were taken against Jagtap and CK summoned Jagtap upon his return to Indore. An enraged CK told Jagtap, "Why did you drink? Get lost". Jagtap still remembers the scolding which he got from CK for his misbehavior. But later on, CK called Jagtap and asked him to get back to cricket. It is worth mentioning here that CK never drank alcohol in his life. Many people had unsuccessfully tried to persuade him to drink. Once, even Maharaja Yashwant Rao on being challenged to make CK drink had failed at the task. At first, Maharaja Yashwant Rao requested CK to drink. When the request did not work, he even threatened CK. But such was CK's willpower, that he did not budge.

Deep inside, CK was a caring man who cared not only for his players but in general for everyone. Long back, Prof. Suryaprakash Chaturvedi (who has written a book on CK in Hindi) had injured his thumb in a practice match at Indore and was scheduled to play an Inter-collegiate match in a couple of days' time. He was tensed and did not know what to do. CK's younger son Prakash Nayudu was Prof. Chaturvedi's friend and he asked the Prof. to come to his house. As Prof. Chaturvedi entered the house he saw CK at the door and as per the Prof. his pain increased out of fear of the great man. CK examined the injury and commanded Prof. Chaturvedi to sit on the chair. He then began the fomentation with his ultraviolet rays machine. It was very painful for the Prof., but CK asked him not to move for half an hour. Recounting that, Prof says, "And this was Col. Nayudu's order, so I closed my eyes and remained seated. Tears were rolling from my eyes but the fear of Col. Nayudu compelled me to obey him". Much to Prof's surprise, after half an hour, his thumb injury seemed half gone and it looked that he could play the match. At the end CK told him, "Look, I want you to play". Prof. Chaturvedi acknowledges CK's gesture which seemed harsh back then but proved to be beneficial in the end.

Another important aspect of CK's captaincy was his field placing. In the game of cricket, field placing is a crucial task performed by a captain. One needs to have a good reading of the game in order to put the right field placement. It is said that a captain has to be lucky, but in addition to it I would say that he has to be a good strategist. In this respect, CK was an excellent strategist who could plan out the dismissals of the opposition batsmen by his imaginative field placements.

As a captain, CK was a very shrewd student of the game. Talking about CK's captaincy, Prof. Chaturvedi recalls a match which CK's team was playing against the Commonwealth Overseas Cricket Team in Indore. Frank Worrell who was also one of CK's favorite cricketer cover drove Hiralal Gaikwad for a boundary. For the very next ball, CK positioned himself at short cover and Gaikwad again bowled a juicy half-volley outside the off stump. Worrell attempted to repeat the cover drive but the ball ended up in the hands of a diving CK who held the catch on to his body. Similarly, one time he had foxed one of India's all-time great Polly Umrigar by removing the fielder at covers. CK had then persisted with his field placing even after the bowler was hit for few boundaries. The end result was that Polly was dismissed for a low score. There are several such stories when the opposition batsmen fell prey to CK's clever captaincy. This just shows that the reputation of the batsman or the situation of the match could not deter CK's attacking instincts as a skipper. As per Vijay Nayudu, CK had a very simple mantra in cricket-"Run banao aur opposition ko out kar do" (Make runs and dismiss the opposition).

On certain instances, CK's mere presence on the cricket field could bring about a change in the opposition team's strategy. Like in the Ranji Trophy final in 1951-52 between Holkar and Bombay, Madhav Apte did not opt for a runner despite having cramps because of the fear of CK. Apte had just recovered from jaundice and was declared fit enough to play in the finals. When batting in the 60s he started getting cramps and told his partner Madhav Mantri, "George I am getting cramps". Mantri replied, "We will slow the running down. But don't take a runner. CK is watching and Indian team is due to get selected". Apte continued playing till 98 with great pain and was eventually out to the bowling of Chandu Sarwate. Apte tells in the end, "But had it not been for CK, Mantri would have recommended a runner for me".

CK's unique and attacking style of captaincy remained the same irrespective of the team that he led. Though he didn't taste success as the captain of the Indian team, but there was never a change in his approach. People say that there wasn't a defensive bone in his body. During a match in 1932, when he had not kept a fielder at third man position and was asked the reason behind it, he replied, "Why should my bowler bowl short pitched ball and that too outside the off stump? So, that the batsman gets a chance to cut?"

For the records, CK led India in four test matches, losing three and drawing one. But then there were other factors which would have contributed to his dismal captaincy record for India. For starters, when he led India, the country was just a new entrant to test match cricket. (India won its first test match in 1952 against England at Madras, 20 years after making debut) Also, CK may not have got a free hand while leading the Indian team due to the high influence of Maharajas in Indian cricket at that time. His fans often speculate that his captaincy record might have been different had he got a longer run leading India. Now, I will refrain myself from commenting on this hypothesis, but I will say that his performance as captain of the Indian team cannot be rated on the basis of such a short stint.

In my humble opinion, his record while leading the Holkar team speaks for itself about his captaincy skills. It is also true that prima facie it seemed as though the other ten players in the Holkar team were supposed to follow whatever CK told them. But then, in CK's defense, wasn't that expected from a player who was decades senior to most of the people in the team? He was probably Indian cricket's first superstar and his role was to mentor the Holkar team. Yes, he may have adopted an uncompromising approach in building his team. But his intentions were right and he did achieve phenomenal success with the same.

Secret behind Colonel's longevity

My statement about several players in the Holkar team being decades junior to CK would have left you wondering about the stretch of CK's cricketing career. Well, the answer is that the time elapsed between CK's first and last first-class match is a mind boggling 47 years. This puts him at the top of the list of people having the maximum span in first-class cricket. WG Grace comes a close second with a first-class career lasting for 44 years. Out of these 47 years, CK played regularly for close to four decades. As stated earlier, he made his first-class debut in 1916 in the Bombay Triangular and made his last Ranji Trophy appearance in 1956-57. His swan song was in a charity match at the age of 68 years in 1963 when he represented Maharashtra Governor's XI against the Maharashtra Chief Minister's XI.

CK had seen a generation of cricketers make their debut and retire, while he went on. I got the best manifestation of CK's long career during my rendezvous with former Indian star Salim Durani. He told me that in addition to himself, his father Abdul Aziz Durani had also played with CK. To play with a father-son duo would be a unique distinction in itself for CK. Abdul Aziz Durani was a wicket-keeper and had played with CK in the second unofficial test between India and Australia in 1935-36 at Kolkata. Before partition, he moved to Pakistan (while Salim and his mother stayed back in India) and became famous as the person to have coached the great Hanif Mohammad.

Salim Durani fondly remembers his first meeting with CK which happened during the 1956-57 Ranji Trophy match between Uttar Pradesh & Rajasthan at Banaras (now Varanasi). He said,

"We had heard a lot about the great Col. CK Nayudu and were very eager to see him. Our manager took us to meet him and we touched his feet upon meeting to seek his blessings". Introducing Salim, the team manager said to CK, "Ye Salim hai. Durani" (He is Salim Durani). CK's response was, "Durani to mera friend tha" (Durani was my friend). The manager replied, "Aziz Durani ka ladka hai" (He is Aziz Durian's son). CK was pleased to hear this and then blessed Salim by putting his hand over Salim's head. He further inquired about the well-being of Salim's mother. Incidentally, this was CK's last appearance in a Ranji Trophy Match. He scored 84 runs before getting run out and the highlight of his innings were the sixes that he hit off the bowling of Vinoo Mankad. Salim Durani who had witnessed this live told me, "It looked as if a 20 years old batsman was playing". Salim Durani regrets that he doesn't have any photo of that match with CK. In years to come, Salim Durani went on to play the same aggressive brand of cricket which CK had advocated. He came to be known as India's on-demand six hitter, who could hit sixes at the demand of the crowd. And CK would have definitely enjoyed his friend's son playing the type of cricket which he had always prescribed. In 1964, while doing commentary for a match in Kanpur, referring to Salim, CK had said, "Salim is trying to connect to the planets". In that match, Salim Durani had scored a flamboyant half-century in just 29 minutes. Returning to CK's last innings in Ranji Trophy, the thing that astonished anyone watching CK bat for this first time would be that if this person is so good at the age of 62 then how good he would have been in his younger days.

Former Indian cricketer Madhav Apte was although not present during CK's last match but he too concurs with this view. Recalling his first real encounter with CK in the 1951-52 Ranji Trophy finals between Holkar & Bombay, Apte says, "I thought if a man can bat like this at the age of 57, then how good he would have been in his prime". This match also witnessed an incident which got added in the list of anecdotes about CK. Apte was standing at the boundary line when CK walked out to the center. Vinoo Mankad who was in the Bombay team, although admired CK as a player but at the same time hated the guts of CK. So, Vinoo bhai as he was called, walked up to fast bowler Dattu

Phadkar who was bowling from the northern end and apparently told him,"Buddhe ko bouncer daal" (Bowl a bouncer to the old man). Given the disdain attitude that CK had towards fast bowlers, both Mankad & Phadkar had guessed that CK would soon step out to hit the fast bowler. As expected, CK stepped out on the third ball and was hit on the mouth. Two teeth came out and his mouth was full of blood. Everyone came running around out of concern. But CK being the man that he was, shooed everyone away. He spat the tooth and took stance to continue his innings, refusing any medical help. He even told the bowler, "Dattu, I am fine, do not help up". Thus, ensuring that Dattu doesn't slow up his pace out of concern for the old man. Despite the injury CK went on to score 66 runs before being bowled to the bowling of Vinoo bhai. CK did not bat in the second innings and Bombay went on to win the match comfortably. However, with his lionhearted outlook, CK had yet again shown that age was just a number as far as he was concerned. He had proved that not even blood could win over his daredevil attitude and take him away from the cricket field. As per CK, the aggression of a batsman needed to visible in his walk to the crease. Explaining how one should go to the wicket, he had said to Vijay Nayudu, "Walk into the wicket as if you are going to the battle field. Look into the eyes of the opposition". He demanded the same kind of fearlessness from his players as well. Rajsingh Dungarpur has written about a match when Hiralal Gaikwad was hit on the mouth by his bowling. Hiralal's mouth was bleeding and his teeth were also broken. But a stern looking CK had shouted at Hiralal, "Get up. Is this even quality fast bowling?" This was probably his way to pump-up his players.

Also, this wasn't the first occasion when CK had demonstrated his physical & mental toughness to continue playing despite the pain. In his last test match, played against England in 1936, CK was hit by England skipper Gubby Allen's bouncer just below his heart. But as Vasant Raiji said, "He was a real army man". CK did not even rub his chest and continued playing. The next ball was also a bouncer and this time he hooked the ball to the fence. His innings of 81 runs could not save the match for India but at least denied the Englishmen an innings victory. Even during this match, CK wasn't a young man and was past 40 years of age.

We all know how years later in 1989, a 16-year-old Sachin Tendulkar had refused to leave the ground after being hit on the nose by a Waqar Younis bouncer in Pakistan. Sachin had just said, "Main Khelega" (I will play). So, maybe fearlessness is an attribute which is common to great cricketers. I am sure, watching this act of heroism from Sachin would have pleased CK in heaven.

The other thing which stayed with CK, even in later part of his career, was his strong reflexes. As a result, he preferred fielding in close-in positions. Normally, youngsters who are fearless and have good reflexes are placed at close-in positions like silly mid-off. But then, even though CK was old, his reflexes were still intact. Once while fielding at silly mid-off during the 1952-53 Ranji Trophy finals, he was hit on the shin by a shot from MV Mathe. Recalling that match, Chandu Borde said, "CK didn't even bother to rub his shin. He just asked everyone to carry on". Imagine this in an age when there were no protective gears in cricket and one's respect for CK's bravery increases manifolds. Citing evidence of his strong reflexes, Vijay Nayudu said that CK used to smoke Panama cigarette and on one occasion while showing something to him, the cigarette fell from CK's mouth. But such were CK's reflexes that he caught the cigarette between his two fingers and did not allow it to fall to the ground.

So, was there a magic formula which kept him going on and on? During my research, I asked this question to several people who had known CK and the common point in the answer that I got was "physical fitness". CK did lay a lot of importance to physical fitness. As per Vijay Nayudu, "CK had a very high fitness level. In today's language we can say that he had a six pack". In order to remain fit, CK used to involve himself in other sports like High Jump, Horse riding etc. His house 'Suraj Kothi' also had two tennis courts. From time to time, CK used to challenge his fitness. One instance when this happened was when he was invited for the inauguration of a college function. He was watching the High Jump finals along with other dignitaries. Suddenly, he expressed the desire to participate in it for fun and asked the benchmark to be increased by 1.5 feet. Much to everyone's surprise, CK cleared the increased mark and that too dressed in formal attire.

Now, physical fitness is a basic necessity in order to have a long career as CK had. But the other aspect which is of paramount importance in such a career is mental toughness. The desire or passion to play has to be there. Unless, one has a deep love for the game, it is impossible to play for such a long span of time. CK possessed all these qualities and these helped him play active cricket for close to half a century. People also sometimes question, if an older player is taking the place of a deserving youngster. We have seen these questions emerge time and again. But as Madhav Apte said, "One should ask a simple question - Will I be depriving a youngster a place in the team? But if I am good enough to compete with the youngster, then there is no reason as to why only age should come in front". And I would guess that in the case of CK, there never was a question on his performance or the value that he brought to the team. Just to give you a perspective of his performances during the later stages of his career, the 200 which he scored against Baroda in the final of the 1945-46 Ranji Trophy at the age of 50 years and 142 days made him the oldest Indian cricketer to have scored a double hundred in first class cricket. Not only this, with this double century he also became the fifth oldest double centurion in all first-class cricket, after Dave Nourse, John King, Archie MacLaren and Jack Hobbs.

CK's long and eventful cricket career is a lesson in itself for every aspiring Indian cricketer. His career had everything which a cricketer can dream of achieving and is relevant even in today's age. It might astonish many that CK was the first Indian cricketer to endorse a brand. He endorsed a brand called Bathgate Liver Tonic in 1941. Reflecting on CK's career, Salim Durani tells that CK's story should be told to the young cricketers. He said, "Usse prerna milegi" (People will seek inspiration from it). He even suggested that such education series about great cricketers of yesteryears should be part of the training regime for small kids.

On their part, the BCCI has tried to keep alive CK's legacy. The Under-23 domestic tournament in India is named as the Col. CK Nayudu Trophy. But the greatest tribute by the BCCI to CK is the naming of the 'Lifetime achievement award' after him. This award was instituted in 2006 to honour people for their contribution to Indian cricket. Since then stalwarts of Indian cricket like Chandu Borde, Nari Contractor, Gundappa Vishwanath, Mohinder Amarnath, Salim Durani, Ajit Wadekar, Sunil Gavaskar, Kapil Dev and Dilip Vengsarkar among others have received this prestigious award.

These prominent names of Indian cricket consider it as a privilege to get an award which has CK's name on it. Chandu Borde who was one of the first recipients of the Col. CK Nayudu Lifetime Achievement Award said, "I was very much elated and happy that I got this award. At the same time, I am very happy that the BCCI has recognized CK's work. It is a great tribute to the person and the game of cricket". Another recipient of this award, Salim Durani said, "Unke naam ka award. Kabhi socha nahin tha ki ye milega. Itni khushi hui thi ki bol nahin sakta" (I had never thought that I will get an award named after him. I cannot tell how much happy I was).

The Administrator

Post retirement from international cricket, CK continued to guide youngsters in domestic cricket. Playing alongside CK was the best learning that young budding Indian cricketers could have asked for. But the phenomenon named CK had a lot more to offer to Indian cricket than just being a cricketer. Given his experience of playing with different players across eras, it would have been a loss to Indian cricket if it had not availed the services of CK's vast knowledge base after his playing days.

So, CK made a smooth transition from being a cricketer to an administrator. He got involved with the BCCI in various capacities, the most noteworthy among them was as a selector. As indicated earlier, during his time with the Holkar team, CK was responsible for handpicking many players from across the country for the Holkar team. Great players like Capt. Mushtaq Ali were CK's find. So, the most natural switch for him from a player was to get involved in the selection of the Indian team. He eventually did that and in fact went on to become the Chairman of Selection Committee of the Indian national team.

In the game of cricket, selectors do play an important role and to have a person of CK's level in the selection committee was a boon for Indian cricket. But, as a selector too, he had his own odd ways of judging the worth of players. He was a person who would not take anything at face value and instead believed in experiencing it himself. So, if a bowler seemed to be bowling fast, he would get a feel of the speed of the ball by facing it himself. He had immense confidence in his own capabilities and more often than not, he could decipher the quality of a player on the basis of his one-on-one in the nets. How much ever bizarre it may sound, the players had to face the chairman of selectors in the nets before getting selected for the Indian team.

Chandu Borde recounts an incident which took place during a test match at Ferozshah Kotla in New Delhi. Some of the rising cricketers had been called by the selectors on the rest day as a part of talent spotting for the next generation. Borde who was an up-coming cricketer had also been invited. This was his first meeting with CK, who was then the chairman of the selection committee. Borde tells, "CK had a towering personality and when he walked in holding a pipe in his mouth, we all were very much impressed by his walk." The invitees were asked to stand in a queue. CK who always had a liking for fast bowlers, first asked the fast bowlers to get into the nets. To everyone's surprise CK took the gloves and came to the nets to bat without the pads. The fast bowlers were confused as they had never experienced anything like this before. In front of them was a great batsman of his times, who was also the current chairman of selectors. Borde adds on, "The fast bowlers were confused whether they should go all-out or bowl slow". In a state of utter disbelief, they bowled two to three deliveries at a slower pace at CK. A furious CK called them and said, "Are you guys fast bowlers? Bowl fast if you want to get selected". So, the bowlers then increased their pace. CK faced these bowlers who were bowling with the new ball without any discomfort. Everyone present out there was stunned at this stunt of CK.

Now, if the batsmen who were present were thinking that they were safe, then they were soon to be proven wrong. After assessing the bowlers, he asked the batsmen to take strike and took the ball himself. He started bowling bouncers to them at shoulder height. Borde who now got a chance to display his talent, played few shots down the line which impressed CK. He immediately called Borde and inquired, "From where are you?" Upon hearing that Borde was from Baroda, CK said, "Now I know why you played like that. You are from the land of Vijay Hazare". CK had played against Hazare in the Bombay Pentangulars and the Ranji Trophy. Hazare, later on, also represented the Holkars for some time. Coincidentally, years later Chandu Borde also went on to become the chairman of selectors for the Indian national team. Though, as a selector he did not adopt CK's ways, but it had left a lasting impression on him.

This wasn't the only instance when CK as a selector had decided to rub shoulders with the probable Indian players in the nets. Prof. Suryaprakash Chaturvedi narrates an incident when former Indian fast bowler Ramakant Desai had been at the receiving end of CK's selection methods. It so happened that Ramakant Desai had come for the trials of the Indian team during CK's tenure as the chairman of selectors. CK took a bat and asked Desai to bowl at him. Like the other contenders who had experienced this unmatched technique of CK, poor Desai didn't know what to do. CK was without leg guards and Desai may not have wanted to injure the chairman of selectors. As a result, he cut down his pace and bowled a bit slowly to CK. But CK knew that Desai could bowl quicker than what he was currently bowling, so he asked him to bowl fast. A nervous Desai somehow managed to bowl a yard quicker, but remained tensed throughout. Such acts were unheard of in the pre or post CK era. This manner of operation was unique to him and probably that's why the great Vijay Merchant had once said that there will never be Nayudu's equal amongst Indians.

CK could do things which were unthinkable for everyone else. He was as unpredictable as one could get. The only person who could probably guess what was going on in CK's mind was CK himself. Once, in a local match in Indore; by the time CK had reached the ground the match had got over. When he asked how the match got finished so early, he was told that a bowler named Bhagwandas had created havoc by taking seven wickets. CK's calm response was, "Main kheloonga use" (I will play him). So, Bhagwandas was called on to bowl to the great CK. One can imagine the mental state of a bowler who had to again bowl after winning the match for his team. Nevertheless, CK being CK, no one dared to question him. CK played him for few deliveries and then hit a beautiful cover drive. He then looked satisfied and told Bhagwandas, "Yes, you bowl well".

One may ponder as to what CK was trying to achieve with

these eccentric ways of operation. Since, CK is no longer with us, we can just speculate the actual reason. One obvious reason could be that he himself was a good cricketer and knew the game inside out. His supreme fitness levels had also meant that he was still competing in domestic cricket with players much younger to him. So, in that sense, he was abreast with the latest trends in the game. But in my opinion, more than technique or anything else, CK may have been trying to test the attitude of these budding cricketers. Just to see how they respond to new situations. On the cricket field every moment brings in a new challenge and CK may have been just trying to simulate the same. Like Chandu Borde said, that as a selector there were many facets of a player that he looked in to. Along with talent and fitness, overall attitude towards the game is very important. Without the right attitude, it is very difficult to succeed as a cricketer or for that matter in any sphere of life.

Along with using these unconventional modus operandi as a selector, in certain matters CK was very headstrong and uncompromising. The reason behind this as Prof Suryaprakash Chaturvedi said was that, "CK judged people from his own high height and pedestal". It may seem that this could have been one of the reasons which transpired an ugly incident in 1952 which Indian cricket could have done without. Now, yet again, we don't know what could have been the real cause or the circumstances back then, but what ensued left a lot of unanswered questions. The Indian cricket team was supposed to tour England in 1952 and CK was the chairman of selection committee. CK had made it mandatory for players to attend the selection trials in order to be considered for selection. During the same time, Vinoo Mankad had got a contract from Haslington Cricket Club in Lancashire league to play as a professional. Vinoo was asked to come back to India for the trials if he wanted to be a part of touring party to England. Vinoo said that he would be penalized if he came back to India as he was playing there as a professional. So, the only condition on which he would come back was if he was promised selection in the Indian team for England. He would then refuse the county contract and come back to serve his nation. To this CK's response was , "When I can't be sure of myself, how can I assure you a place in the team". He was not impressed by Vinoo's request. He went on to tell everyone that India had many more players like Vinoo Mankad and the team was not dependent on an individual. CK's famous lines were, "We can produce a dozen Vinoo Mankads". Just to give a perspective of this bold statement, one may recall that in the early 1950s Vinoo Mankad was one of the best all-rounders in the world. While, CK's statement was believed to be the stand of the BCCI on this issue. But contrary to popular belief, JC Mukherjee who was then the president of the BCCI had said that strenuous efforts were made by the board to ensure Vinoo Mankad's participation in the tour.

Unfortunately, for the India team, CK had his way and Vinoo Mankad was kept out of the team. Hiralal Gaikwad was selected as the left-arm spinner in place of Mankad. This team led by Vijay Hazare failed miserably in the first test match at Leeds and Mankad's absence was alluded as one of the reasons behind the team's lamentable performance. Barring Vijay Hazare and Vijay Merchant, none of the Indians had answers to the questions posed by the English bowlers. Hazare scored 89 runs and Merchant went on to score a century. In response, the Englishmen took a lead of 41 runs. But the second innings brought in more disaster for the Indians. At one stage in the second innings, the Indian team had lost four wickets without a run on the board. Hazare and Dattu Phadkar (who scored 64 runs) saved India from an embarrassment by putting together a century partnership for the sixth wicket. The England team were set a target of 125 runs in the fourth innings. This was achieved easily and India eventually lost the match by seven wickets.

This loss sent down ripples in the Indian team management. As if to add salt to injury, Vinoo performed brilliantly for the Haslington Cricket Club during the same time. In a bid to bring the situation under control, Indian captain Vijay Hazare sent a cable to the BCCI to grant him permission to include Vinoo Mankad for the remaining tests. It is also said that the Indian team manager, Pankaj Gupta had played a key part in Hazare sending this SOS to the BCCI. Pankaj Gupta was a strong-willed man himself and had been the manager of the Olympics Gold winning Indian Hockey team. He was also the coach of legendary Hockey player Dhyan

Chand and is often credited with giving the title of "Chand" (Dhyan Chand's original name was Dhyan Singh). In this controversy surrounding Vinoo Mankad's readmission to the team, Pankaj had said that he always had the prestige of the country in mind and by including Vinoo in the team he was not by any means bringing down India's prestige. On their part, the Haslington Cricket Club also agreed to release Mankad. So, after all this drama, Vinoo Mankad eventually joined the team for the second test in Lord's. This match is often labelled as the "Mankad test", not because of the controversy but due to his superlative all-round performance. Mankad scored 72 &184 runs in the two innings and also took five wickets in England's first innings. Madhav Apte who although wasn't part of the Indian team, but had travelled to England on his own to be with the team had witnessed this match. He said that it looked as though Vinoo Mankad was in the form of his life. He was having a purple patch and when you are in that phase nothing goes wrong. But despite Mankad's heroic, India lost the match by 8 wickets. In retrospect, had it not been for Mankad's performance, India might well have lost the match by an innings. So it is fair to conclude that Vinoo's return had definitely boosted the performance of the team. Vinoo played the remaining two tests as well but could not help the Indians in reversing the fortunes and India lost the series 0-3.

If this was happening on the field, more drama was ensuing off the field. CK had resigned from the selection committee as he was not happy with the team management's decision to include Vinoo Mankad in the team. This may have been the first high-profile resignation in Indian cricket. Given the strict disciplinarian that CK was, I am sure he would never have given a go-ahead for Vinoo's inclusion. For, CK's belief was that a rule shouldn't be bent for anyone. The stature of the player or the circumstances could not come in between the implementation of his commandment.

Thankfully for Indian cricket, sanity prevailed and CK returned back to the selection committee after a season. Some people say that CK had later on realized that the action taken by the team management was in the best interest of Indian cricket. There isn't any strong evidence suggesting that this was the truth other than the fact that he returned back to the selection committee. As far as Vinoo Mankad was concerned, he too was not pleased at the treatment meted out to him and in fact had also considered retirement. But as they all is well that ends well. Both CK and Mankad continued to serve Indian cricket in their different capacities for many more years. Many people say that this episode was the main reason for the sourness of relationship between CK and Mankad. Now, it may not be right for me to comment on the harmony or lack of it between CK & Vinoo Mankad. But as Vinoo's son Rahul Mankad (also a first-class cricketer) said that hatred may not be the right word to define their relationship. Vinoo Mankad admired CK for his longevity, but at the same time hated CK's toughness.

This incident apart, CK's association with Indian cricket post his playing days brought in good results. There were people whom he would have disliked, but that never stopped him from openly acknowledging their good qualities. Rajsingh Dungarpur once wrote that CK and Lala Amarnath did not have the best of the relations. But even then, when Rajsingh had asked him to choose the best amongst Vijay Hazare, Vijay Merchant and Lala Amarnath, CK's response was that Lala would triumph even if both the Vijays were combined together.

At times, his resoluteness could bring the best out of players. Like, it happened in the test match between India and England in 1951 at Bombay when the Indian captain Vijay Hazare had been hit on the eyebrow while attempting a hook shot. Hazare had come to the dressing room to get a stitch and seeing him, CK enquired what the batsman was doing in the dressing room. Hazare told him that he was getting his wound treated. To this CK replied, "It can wait". So, the Indian skipper had to go back to the middle much against his wish. Ironically, Hazare ended up scoring 155 runs and emerged as the highest scorer in the Indian innings. Now, whether it was CK's words which had pepped Hazare to perform is something that I will not dwell on.

But I can't imagine any administrator or for that matter any person meting out this kind of a treatment to the captain of the Indian cricket team. Then this wasn't just any administrator, this was CK. He commanded such a position of reverence in Indian cricket that even the skipper of the national team could not question him. His contribution to Indian cricket was recognized by the government and the board at different points in time. His 50th birthday was celebrated with much fanfare in Bombay and Calcutta. The government of India honored him with the Padma Bhushan award, the third highest civilian award in 1956. This made him the first cricketer to be awarded with the prestigious award. On his 60th birthday, Dr. S Radhakrishna, the then Vice President of India, presented him with another award and a road was named after him at his birthplace Nagpur.

Last Session

As they say, life is not all about sunshine and rainbows, the story of CK's life in the later stages was not all about just these awards and recognitions. Sadly, in the last few years of his life, he too had to face things like hatred and isolation from the people in charge of the cricketing matters. It might seem strange that how could a man of such repute be meted out with ill-treatment. But then, when one has ruled the game for so long as CK had done, one is bound to have a few haters as well. Add to it CK's uncompromising attitude and we have the perfect breeding ground for enemies. It was well-known that many players did hate his insistence on discipline, they couldn't question CK's strictness back then due to his stature. There would have been many people whose ideas would have been out rightly rejected by CK. I am sure these people would have been waiting for their chance to pounce on CK. Given CK's longevity, his detractors had to wait for close to 50 years for their reprisal.

But when they got their opportunity, they ensured that he was humiliated in every possible way. They connived to keep CK out of the game, which had been his life. As a result, this last session in the game called life, for CK, was extremely painful not only for him but for his well-wishers as well. Lamenting on this Prof Suryaprakash Chaturvedi said, "His last days were pathetic because people who had seen him rule on the cricket field like a king had got together to take revenge. They began humiliating and ignoring him. And Col. Nayudu was not prepared for this, because he used to dominate wherever he went."

The cricketing dynamics of Indore was changing. The Holkar era had ended and the cricketing reigns had passed on to people who did not value CK's principles. They did not have place for his strict ways, which had for years been the hallmark of Holkar cricket. CK's words were no longer considered as the final say in cricketing matters in the state. This spree of CK's humiliation started when he was kept out of the cricket association of Madhya Pradesh. Not only was he kept out of it, but no one had even informed him about the formation of such an association. It is said that CK was playing billiards in the Yashwant Club, when the news about the formation of this cricket association reached to him. It would be an understatement to say that he was hurt. But the writing was on the wall and CK could very well read what was being transpired. He was purposefully being kept out of the cricketing affairs of the state and this was unacceptable to him. Similarly, when the stadium was constructed in Indore, it was assumed that it would be named after him. For, he was beyond doubts the greatest sporting son of Indore. But instead, the stadium was named after India's first prime minister, Pandit Jawaharlal Nehru. CK was not accustomed to fight for his name and it was probably not in his nature to do such things. CK knew that some efforts were made by his loyal well-wishers to have the stadium named after him. But when things turned against him, his humble response was, "We are all very proud of our beloved leader of the nation, Jawaharlal Nehru and it should be a matter of pride for us that the Stadium has been named after this great son of India".

The final nail in the coffin came in 1966 when a cricket tournament was organized in memory of the late Maharaja Yashwant Rao Holkar in Indore. The four teams participating in the tournament were - Prof. DB Deodhar's XI, Khandu Rangnekar's XI, Maharaja Yashwant Rao Cricket Club and State Bank of India. The obvious name missing from the list of the teams was a Col. CK Nayudu's XI. It was impossible to believe how the organizers could have overlooked his name. Along with being the great cricketer that he was, his closeness with Maharaja Yashwant Rao was widely known. It was clear that Col. CK Nayudu's XI had been purposefully omitted from the list of the teams. Being the self-respecting man that CK was, he never asked for any explanations on this ill-treatment. Reportedly, Khandu Rangnekar had met CK prior to the start of the tournament. But the exact discussion that happened between the two did not come out in open. On this, his daughter Chandra Nayudu writes, "I was too hurt and pained even to discuss the matter with anyone. I do not know why was father given this raw deal, this unfair treatment; but this much I know, he was a very hurt and a very sad man".

Throughout his life, he had cherished talking about cricket with people. He could spend hours discussing cricket, but even this was changing quickly. Saddened by the turn of events, he built a sort of cocoon around him. He largely constricted himself to his home. So, although his enemies had been successful in taking CK out of cricket, but they still couldn't take cricket out of him. CK still used to listen to the commentary from home. Gradually, the count of visitors at his house also reduced. Only his family members and few loyal friends used to visit him. He still used to attend few functions when invited, but such a somber life was not something that CK was used to.

Things had reached a stage when it was getting too much for CK to digest. All these, coupled with old age was taking a toll on his health and it started deteriorating fast. Vijay Nayudu, who was in Indore with CK during his last days relates an incident when a glass fell from CK's hand during dinner. Now, the falling of a glass may not seem an alarming event for most people. But given the strong grip that CK had, all the family members were stunned. Vijay asked him, "Nana kya ho gaya?" (What happened Nana?). CK did not say anything. Vijay quietly informed this to Dr. SK Mukherjee, who was their family doctor. CK never liked getting examined by doctors or taking medicines. Upon seeing Dr. Mukherjee, the next day, instead of the doctor asking him about his wellbeing, CK asked him, "What happened doc?". It was unimaginable for CK that his health was betraying him. This is understandable as CK used to take great pride in his fitness. And given his aversion to medicines, it was a task in itself to give medicines to him. Vijay was entrusted with his responsibility for a while. As CK was fond of having paan, Vijay and the other family members tried mixing the medicine with his paan. This trick did work for some time and small dosages of medicine was given to CK.

Another incident which shows the extent to which his health

had worsened took place when CK was going to the Commissioner's house along with Vijay in their Dodge car. CK was driving the car and Vijay suddenly noticed that his beloved Nana was unable to gather enough power to even change the gear of the car. So, Vijay asked him if he could drive. In a bid to hide this weakness which he had developed recently, CK did not respond and just took a U-turn to return home. On yet another occasion, while walking with Vijay, CK began to bend. It was Vijay's presence of mind which averted any mishap. As soon as Vijay saw his Nana bending, he got the car and took him home. These developments alarmed Vijay and he informed the same to his mother. The family made every effort to bring back their Nana as they had known them, fit and upright. But the lack of improvement in his health was getting frustrating for them as well.

About old age it is said that, "What makes old age hard to bear is not the failing of one's faculties, mental and physical, but the burden of one's memories". The tall and elegant CK was now only a shadow of his former self. This was agonizing for his family members, who could have never imagined their Nana in such a condition. The memories of his past were making it difficult to accept the reality. The man who in his heydays had spectators thronging the grounds just to see him walk from the pavilion to the pitch, was struggling to even walk properly today. For the last few months of his life, he was confined to bed. Who would have thought that the person who didn't used to allow his children to lie down on bed out of regular times (as he thought it wasn't good for their health), would become so weak one day that to even get up from the bed would become a task for him. At times, he would not even recognize people other than his family members. Once CK was bedridden, his family made a conscious effort to not allow people take his photograph. They did not want the world to have the image of an ailing CK. This was understandable as till now people could only relate to words like 'graceful' with CK. His family did not want the world to have the last image of an old and weak CK.

One thing that was clear for everyone around CK was that in the game of life, very few overs were remaining in his innings. This reminds me of a conversation between CK and Prof Suryaprakash

Chaturvedi that took place years back during a local match. The point of contention was the number of overs left before lunch. Prof. Chaturvedi was the umpire and CK had asked him the time. Prof. Chaturvedi told him that it was the last over before lunch. To this CK shouted, "How do you know? There could be one more over". As it turned out to be, one more over was bowled. Remembering this Prof. Chaturvedi told me, "Col. was right, because I should have just told him the time. It was my mistake". Today, CK's fans were wishing that there could be few more overs in CK's life. Although CK's family members and the doctors were trying their level best to provide him with the right medication, his innings in life was nearing its end.

The fateful day arrived one day after the "Tulsi Lagan' which was normally celebrated in grand style at CK's house. It was the 14th of November, 1967, when Indian cricket's first superstar, at the age of 72 years began his walk to the heavens. I am sure he would have entered the gates of heavens with the same grace as he used to approach the wicket. The news of his demise reached the corners of the country immediately. And people started rushing to his house to pay their final respect. The final journey of his mortal remains was attended by his old teammates like Capt. Mushtaq Ali, Major Jagdale, JN Bhaya, Hiralal Gaikwad and several other fans. But still, the number of people in his final journey were less than what would have been anticipated in the case of a big name like CK. It seemed to many that he had paid the price for his theories and principles.

Nevertheless, there was an outpour of condolences from one and all. One of the most complete messages describing CK was from his disciple Capt. Mushtaq Ali, who had said, " Col. Nayudu's loss is a personal shock to me for he was my guru. I owe my cricket entirely to his guidance and coaching. In the death of Col. Nayudu the 'master of sixes' in his heyday, Indian cricket in particular and international cricket in general has lost one of the most glittering personalities. Indian cricket was rightly proud of the dynamic Captain and the majestic personality, who charmed and captured the hearts of thousands of onlookers and spectators, when, with his kingly gait, he walked from the dressing room to the wicket bat in hand".

Mrs. Indira Gandhi, the then Prime Minister of India had also conveyed her condolences on CK's demise. She had said, "Col. CK Nayudu's contribution to cricket is well-known. A great player himself, he personified the dignity and elegance of the game. By his fine example, he inspired a generation of young cricketers. He had a genius for discovering talent and shaped many of our finest players. The country has lost in him a loveable personality, a true sportsman".

Indeed, the country had lost a true sportsman. But then, as they say that the only certain thing in life is that it will one day end. CK's life had ended, but he had left a legacy behind him. He had achieved a lot in the world of cricket and there was nothing to regret from his cricketing career. Yes, he may have wanted his last session to be a bit more cordial, but one doesn't always get everything in life. And CK had got almost everything. The pied piper of Indore had left the stadium of the earth with his head held high.

The fact that CK shared his birthday with the Iron man of India, Sardar Vallabhbhai Patel (both of them were born on October 31st), has often led to comparisons between the two great men. I would just say that like Sardar Patel was instrumental in getting all the princely states acceded to India, CK also played a crucial role in spotting talent from across the country. And given CK's commitment to Indian cricket, it won't be wrong to call him the "Iron Man of Indian Cricket".

CK with Prof. DB Deodhar - the Grand Old Man of Indian Cricket

CK with Sardar Vallabhbhai Patel

CK with his English counterpart Douglas Jardine

Salim Durani with the prestigious CK Nayudu Lifetime Achievement Award at his house in Jamnagar

The trophy presented to Salim Durani

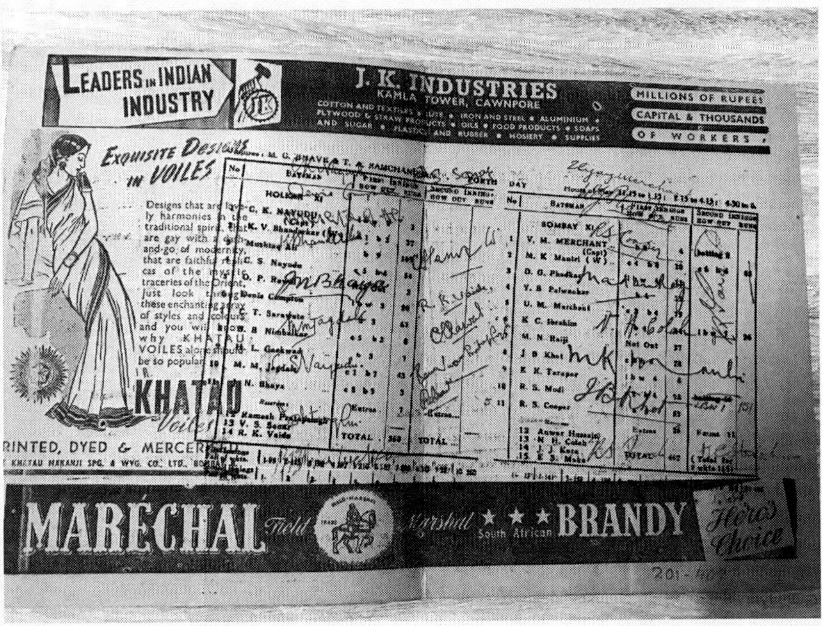

Official scorecard from the Col. Nayudu Golden Jubilee match signed by CK

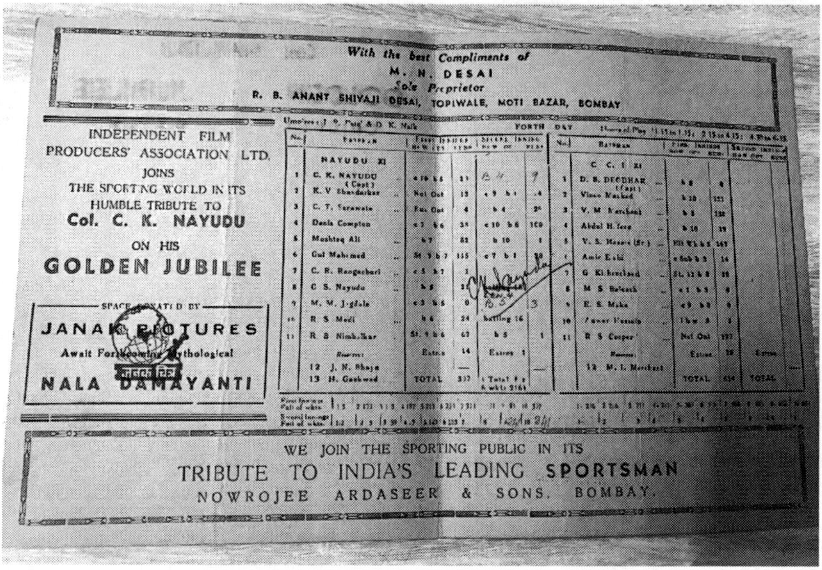
With the best Compliments of
M. N. DESAI
Sole Proprietor
R. B. ANANT SHIVAJI DESAI, TOPIWALE, MOTI BAZAR, BOMBAY

INDEPENDENT FILM PRODUCERS' ASSOCIATION LTD.
JOINS
THE SPORTING WORLD IN ITS
HUMBLE TRIBUTE TO
Col. C. K. NAYUDU
ON HIS
GOLDEN JUBILEE

SPACE DONATED BY
JANAK PICTURES
Await Forthcoming Mythological
NALA DAMAYANTI

FORTH DAY

NAYUDU XI

C. C. I. XI

WE JOIN THE SPORTING PUBLIC IN ITS
TRIBUTE TO INDIA'S LEADING SPORTSMAN
NOWROJEE ARDASEER & SONS, BOMBAY.

Official scorecard from the Col. Nayudu Golden Jubilee match signed by CK

What if?

Now, I am not a big fan of comparing cricketers across different eras or postulating about how a cricketer would have performed in a different epoch. In my view, such comparisons do not do justice to the players involved. Other than the technique and talent of a cricketer, there are many factors like the quality of opposition and the nature of wickets among others which need to be considered for such comparisons. But the truth is that one may never be able to get all the parameters right. So, it may not be always right to assume that a player who was great in one era, would be great in another.

In spite of me holding this viewpoint, in CK's case, the two words that often comes to my mind are 'What if?' What if India was a test playing nation during CK's prime? What if he had not lost so many years due to the World Wars? What if he was allowed to lead India for a few more test matches? What if CK had played Twenty-20 (T20) cricket? 'What If' are two words with endless possibilities. It is rightly said that the 'what-ifs' and the 'should-haves' can eat one's brain. Hence, I will not try to answer all these questions except the last one. Although, I know that the times in which CK played the game was very different from today and even the social environment was different. But still, the last question in particular excites me and the reason behind this fantasy of mine is CK's love for aggression.

Once a young player had asked CK about how one should play bouncers. His response was that it should be played by hitting out of the ground. And it wasn't just talks, he practiced what he preached. Once during a match against Parsi XI, former Indian cricketer Piloo Palia was wreaking havoc with his bowling.

CK, who was watching this from the pavilion was getting restless. He was aghast at the defensive approach taken by his batsmen. As per him, the batsmen should have been hitting Palia. Everyone thought that he was speaking out of his mind. But when CK came to bat, he hit couple of consecutive sixes of the bowling of Palia. Now an in-form Palia was a difficult bowler to contend with, but CK hit him all around the ground. As his former Holkar teammate MK Shukla told, "He had just demonstrated what he had been telling us in the pavilion."

It is worthwhile to remind that CK's first runs in the Bombay Quadrangular had also come by the medium of a six. He rarely used to take time to settle down and would start hitting from the word go. He didn't believe in the traditional approach of giving the first hour to the bowler. If the ball was to be hit, then CK didn't spare it irrespective of the situation of the match. So, in that sense, in today's language, his approach can be called T20 like. I posed my hypothesis about CK and T20 to everyone whom I met during my research phase for this book. I asked them, "Would Col. CK Nayudu have been successful if T20 cricket was played during his time?" Some laughed away at my fanciful notion, few doubted CK's liking for the shorter format; but most of the people were convinced that CK would have been successful in T20 as well.

His grandson, Vijay Nayudu agreed with me and said that CK would have loved to play T20 cricket. As per him, to be an attacking batsman, one's defense should be very strong and CK did have a strong defense as well. He added on to say that CK may not have liked the color clothing associated with T20. CK loved the white cricketing attire and he was very particular about everything being absolutely clean. Vasant Raiji who is a big self-confessed fan of CK, said that he considers test match cricket as real cricket. But when asked to comment on T20 cricket and CK, a smile came on to his face and he said, "Had Colonel Saab played T20 cricket, he would have been number one, hitting all those sixes".

Like Raiji, former Indian test player Madhav Apte also is not a big fan of T20 cricket. Apte nevertheless agrees that it has brought a lot more money into cricket, which is good for the game. It is understandable for these guys to prefer test cricket over T20.

Some say that the beauty of test cricket is that it is one of the few things in life which gives you a second chance. But I will leave the debate between T20 and Test match cricket for another day. Returning to CK and T20 cricket, Apte said, "I can't say if CK would have liked T20 cricket or not. But if there is anybody from that era who would have been appropriate for T20, then it would be CK. What talent he had!" As per Apte, CK was a man made for limited overs cricket. If he had played ODIs or T20s, he would have opened the batting. In addition Apte said, "Watching CK bat, it seemed like that he played with the principle-"Bani to bani nahin to abdul gani" (a phrase which means that he played with a carefree approach). In reality, Apte knows that there was a method to CK's madness. It is indeed credit to CK, that he made batting look so simple.

Salim Durani who himself was famous for hitting sixes on demand got excited on this topic and said, "Had T20 cricket been played during Col. Saab's days, I can't imagine what he would have done. He could have easily taken the team score in the range of 200 to 250 runs". The fact that he could hit the ball so cleanly for long sixes with a bat much smaller and lighter as compared to the ones used today tells a story in itself.

Former Holkar player Waman Jagtap stretched my theory and said that not only CK, but any Holkar player would have succeeded in T20 cricket. The reason for this was that they were all taught to hit from the first ball. About CK he said, "CK would have enjoyed T20 cricket. Bahut maarte agar woh aaj hote (He would have hit a lot, had he been around)". Maybe Jagtap was right, aggression was the only way in which the Holkars knew to play the game. Vijay Nayudu had narrated an incident which speaks a lot about the philosophy of Holkar players. Vijay was finding it difficult to bat on a matting wicket and had gone to Capt. Mushtaq Ali seeking his advice. Mushtaq's response was, "Ball agar stump par hai to maaro" (If the ball is in the line of the stumps, then hit it). It was rare to have this kind of approach in those days. Mushtaq, who has the distinction of being the first Indian to score a test century on foreign soil (he had achieved this feat in 1936 against England at Old Trafford), was himself a dashing and flamboyant batsman. Rightfully, the T20 cricket domestic championship in India, organized by the BCCI is named after him as the Syed Mushtaq Ali Trophy.

The other aspect of T20 which is very much in line with CK's thinking was the emphasis on fielding. Even the biggest critic of T20 cricket will agree that it has helped elevate the standards of fielding. The kind of catches which are taken in T20 cricket today, were considered unthinkable until recently. For instance, the juggling of catches at the boundary line by the same player or between two players is T20's gift to fielding. Even the ground fielding has seen a radical change with the rise of T20 cricket. And one feature common to any successful T20 team around the world is the focus on fielding. In today's age, a poor fielder is often considered as a burden for the team. Though he might score runs or take wickets, but if he leaks away 15-20 runs due to his fielding; it is an irreparable damage to the team.

In this regard, CK or his Holkar team were tailor-made for T20 cricket. Though, their fielding standards may not have been anywhere close to the athleticism displayed by today's teams, the amount of time spent in fielding drills by the Holkar team was unheard of during those days. And in their times, the Holkars were considered a good fielding outfit. This was largely due to the efforts of CK. Recently, Indian captain Virat Kohli had made a comment that he asks his teammates to only do the things which he can himself do. Similarly, CK led by example. He was himself a very good fielder and even in the later part of his career would not be afraid to stand in close-in positions.

Given this stress on fielding or even otherwise, T20 cricket also demands a certain level of fitness. We have seen many cases of how players have been dropped from the team due to their low fitness levels. Yet again, fitness is something that CK insisted a great deal on. CK was a fitness freak and he expected no less from his players. His strong reflexes stayed with him throughout his career and this can be attributed to the importance that he lay on fitness.

Among the people whom I met, the only person who held a different opinion on CK & T20 cricket was Chandu Borde. He refrained from commenting on whether CK would have been a successful T20 cricketer. But he said that he was not too sure if CK would have appreciated T20 cricket a lot. And the reason behind Borde's thinking is the kind of shots that CK played. CK believed in playing with a straight bat and his batting could not be called as slogging. Now it is true that, T20 cricket has given birth to many unorthodox shots. But, I would only say that it is not necessary to slog to be successful in T20s. We have seen many players who have succeeded in the shorter formats despite playing orthodox cricketing shots. Yes, the number of such cricketers are less, but this breed does exist even today. Hence, I see no reason as to why an attacking player like CK wouldn't have cherished T20 cricket. The only part of T20 which I think CK would not have liked is to have defensive fields to save the runs, for he believed in bowling to take wickets rather than containing the runs. In that sense, it would have been interesting to see if he would have actually modified his captaincy style as per the format of the game.

So, leaving apart the question of CK liking T20 cricket or not and his captaincy, the general consensus that I got was that he would have definitely been successful in the shorter formats. His aggressive batting, the importance given to fielding and fitness, all seem to suggest that CK and T20 would have been a happy couple. CK was a game-changer, an entertainer and a crowd puller. These are the qualities which one expects from a player who wants to be successful in T20 cricket today.

To give a history of T20 cricket, it came into existence 36 years after CK's death when an inter-county competition was introduced by the England and Wales Cricket Board (ECB) in 2003. And the Indian cricket team's T20 journey began three years later on December 1st, 2006 with a victory against South Africa at Johannesburg. Coincidently, 80 years back, it was on the same day in December on which CK had plundered the MCC attack during his innings of 153 at the Bombay Gymkhana. That knock by Indian cricket's first superstar had announced the arrival of Indian cricket to the world. So, in my opinion, there couldn't have been a better day to start Indian cricket's T20 voyage. Now, this might not have been planned by the organizers, but I wonder if there was a divine hand governing all this. Maybe, this was destiny's way of telling us that T20 cricket in India had the blessings of CK.

T20 cricket itself has come a long way in the country since 2006. The victory of the Indian team in the 2007 T20 World Cup and the advent of the Indian Premier League (IPL) have taken it to a different level altogether. Today, the IPL is the richest cricket league in the world and players from across the globe take part in it. This has also given an opportunity to young Indian players to rub shoulders with international stars. And this has reflected on the performance of the Indian team in T20.

However, the IPL which has city based teams, does not yet feature a team from CK's City of Indore. And the greedy cricket fan in me wishes that we have a 'CK's Indorians' in future, as a mark of respect to the great man. Whether my desire is fulfilled or not, happens to be seen. But in my mind, if T20 cricket is taken back in time to CK's era, then he would have been one of the most celebrated cricketer in the format. Be it the audacity to hit from the beginning or strong reflexes while fielding, CK was blessed with all the qualities needed to succeed at T20 cricket.

The Nayudus

Till now we have only seen the cricketing side of CK. So, how was CK at home? What was his family background? I got answers to these and many more from his family members.

Originally, the Nayudus hailed from Krishna district in Andhra Pradesh. CK's great grandfather then moved to Hyderabad, where he was an interpreter to the Nizam. It was his grandfather, C. Narayanswamy who made Nagpur, the home of the Nayudus. He studied law there and became a well-known lawyer in the city. He was also a landlord and one of the initial members of the All-India National Congress party.

CK's father, Cottari Suryaprakashrao Nayudu followed in the footsteps of his father and also became a lawyer. Though, Suryaprakashrao went to the University of Cambridge in England to study law, he returned back to Nagpur and continued his practice there. With his return from the British Islands, he also brought in the game of cricket to the city of oranges. The Nayudus are considered as the trailblazers of cricket in the city. And as stated earlier, it is in this city of Central India, that Indian Cricket's first test captain, CK was born. He spent the early years of his life in the city, before the game of cricket took him first to Bombay and then to Indore.

Today, if you ask anyone, they would say that CK was from Indore. As it is said in Hindi, Indore became CK's 'Karmabhoomi' (the land where one works). The time in Indore was probably the most fruitful period of CK's life. His children consider the days spent at their house, 'Suraj Kothi' in Indore to be the best of their life. CK had nine children from his two marriages (His first wife, Chandramma had passed away only a few years post their wedding) , seven girls and two sons. As his son Prakash has jokingly written in his book, along with their father and mother, they comprised the Col. CK Nayudu XI.

Indore proved to be lucky for CK in cricketing matters as well. It was during this time that he became the captain of the Indian team and then later on led the Holkar team to greater heights. But, given his cricketing engagements, was he able to devote some time at home? Was the discussion at the home of the Nayudus always about cricket?

If you were wondering whether the strict disciplinarian CK had imposed a military rule at home, then his daughter Leela Vidyasagar's comments gave us an insight. She said, "My father really was a perfect example of discipline, in everything we had to follow rules." Excerpts from Chandra Nayudu's book also suggest the same. Explaining CK's love affair with discipline, she has written, "Discipline was the ruling factor of his life and our Nana had not only imposed self-discipline on himself, but expected the same discipline from us". Sanjay Jagdale, who as a young boy used to go to CK's house with his father said that he too feared CK. CK's personality was such that it scared him.

His grandson Vijay Nayudu, who also had the privilege of staying with him for some time elaborates this and says that everyone had to be back home in time in the evening. The rule was to be home before sunset. And knowing the infamous temper of CK, rarely did anyone take the chance of returning late. Once, Vijay as a school kid in Indore, got late. In a bid to escape the wrath of his Nana, he made a plan to enter through the back gate. But as luck would have had it, upon entering he saw CK standing in front of him. CK asked him, "Why so late today?". A nervous Vijay replied, "There was a cricket match and hence I got late. We won the match and I scored 132 runs." Most of the grandparents would have been happy at this and would have praised their wards. But being the perfectionist that CK was, he asked Vijay, "How did you get out?". So, while Vijay had been spared for coming late, now there was another explanation that he had to give. Just envisage a school kid having to describe about how he had been dismissed to India's first test captain and that too after having scored a century. It is a different matter, that to Vijay, CK was just his Nana and not the great Col. CK Nayudu. But if CK had asked a question then it warranted a reply, irrespective of who you were. So, poor Vijay replayed his dismissal to his Nana. CK then showed Vijay, how the shot had to be played which wouldn't have resulted in his wicket. A detailed discussion followed and it stopped only when CK was convinced that the analysis of Vijay's dismissal had been done to his satisfaction. Once the cricketing matters were resolved, the softer side of CK came out. He asked Vijay to come back after taking a bath. Vijay took his own time to freshen up and assumed that his Nana would have had his dinner. But to his surprise, when he came back, his Nana was waiting for him at the dinner table. The two then had dinner together and even today Vijay fondly remembers this incident.

These gestures might seem small to many people, but it tells a lot about the personality of CK. While on one hand, CK the cricketer was trying to teach a youngster few finer points of the game and on the other hand, the grandfather in CK was affectionately waiting for Vijay at the dinner table. Such a blend of toughness and tenderness is rare to be found. This was not the only instance when CK passed on his cricketing wisdom to Vijay. He often used to guide Vijay in cricketing matters. Once, when he was not happy with Vijay's defense, he asked Vijay to get a bat and get ready to face him. CK bowled and Vijay defended, but the ball went towards CK. Unhappy at the defense, CK said, "Ball yahin rukna chahiye (Ball should stop here)". He then took the bat and demonstrated the proper manner in which the ball should be defended. Talking about CK's greatness Vijay tells, "Of course, I am proud to be his grandson and I always wanted to play like him. Lekin bahut late maloom pada unke baare mein (Came to know very late about his greatness)". This also shows that, at home CK's feet were grounded and he tried to be as normal as possible. He was fond of writing letters to his family members despite his busy schedule. In one of the letters addressed to Vijay, he congratulated him for starting his schooling and regretted that he wasn't there to see his grandson write his first alphabets.

He was a typical father or head of the family who was not prepared to allow his children to take any shortcuts in life. So, all the children at the house of the Nayudus had to take part in the household activities. Be it painting of the doors, polishing furniture or gardening, these chores were part of the upbringing of every child at their house. Since, he owned a car at a time when only the rich and the famous could afford one, it was natural for his children to develop a liking for driving as they grew up. But here too, learning to drive was not a straight forward affair at the house. As Vijay said, “Before trying our hands at driving, we had to learn other aspects related to the car. We first had to learn to wash the car properly and put air in the tyres. Only then Nana would allow us to get started with driving”. This is a stark departure from the usual life of kids of famous people, who are often served with most things directly on their plate.

In his children, CK inculcated the virtue that everything in life had to be earned. His eldest son, Bobji got to learn this the hard way. One time, when CK was out of town, Bobji wore CK’s India blazer and took the car to roam with his friend Waman Jagtap. When Bobji came back, he wasn’t expecting his father to be at home. But CK had returned one day earlier than expected. On seeing Bobji wearing his India blazer, a fuming CK said, “Do you know what color is this? Take off the blazer and bring the scissors.” He then cut the logo of the Indian cricket team on the blazer and giving it back to Bobji he angrily said, “You should only wear the blazer of the Indian cricket team, when you deserve it.” Jagtap recalled that like Bobji, he too had invited CK’s anger when he had got stitched a pullover of the same color as worn by the Indian team. Noticing Jagtap with the pullover, CK had said, “This is the color of the Indian team. Hopeless fellow, remove it. You are not supposed to wear it”. And Jagtap had promptly removed the pullover. So, CK had the same barometer for everyone. He did not grant any concessions to his children or close relatives.

CK was also very particular about his clothes. His driver, Dhanna had the responsibility of keeping his shoes, pants and shirts ready, by the time CK took a bath. All his clothes were kept neatly hanging in his room. On even the days when CK was at home, he had a set routine. He would browse through various newspapers while having tea. Leela Vidyasagar smiles and says that there used to be at least six different newspapers which he

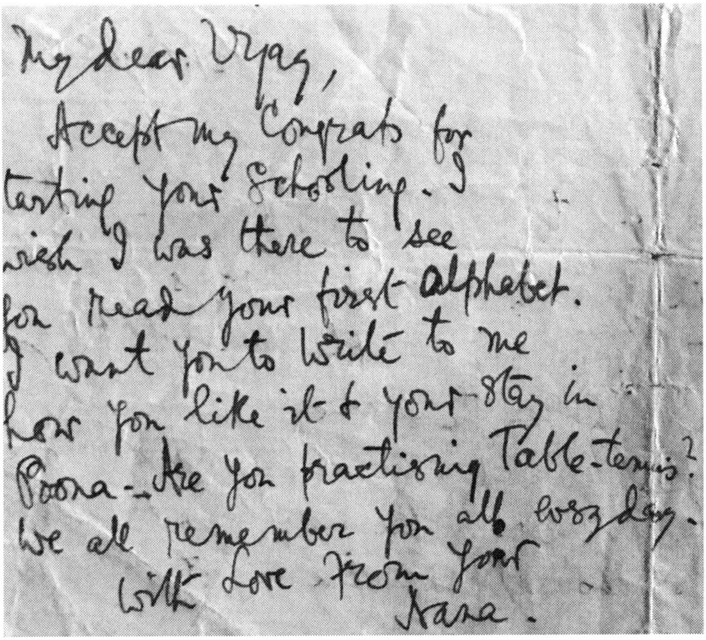
My dear Vijay,
Accept my Congrats for
starting your schooling. I
wish I was there to see
you read your first alphabet.
I want you to write to me
how you like it & your stay in
Poona. Are you practising Table-tennis?
We all remember you all every day.
With Love from your
Nana.

The letter written by CK to his grandson Vijay Nayudu

would scan. After reading the newspapers, he would take bath and then proceed towards the pooja room. The light would already be lit there for him and he used to meditate there for 10 minutes. This was followed by breakfast, before settling in the verandah to meet and greet the visitors. If CK would have been a king, then his verandah was his court where he entertained all the visitors irrespective of their social status. The list of visitors to his court would range from the Maharaja to a poor civilian.

With so much of action happening at the house, there was an immense responsibility on the lady of the house to run it smoothly. And CK's second wife, Gunawati did ensure that the domestic affairs were handled properly. She was the backbone of the house who saw to it that her husband could peacefully concentrate solely on cricketing matters. She was a very humble lady who cared for one and all. Looking back at the contribution of her mother in the Nayudu household, Leela Vidyasagar says, "She was a loving wife and a devoted mother. She never craved for anything and was happy in herself. I owe my life to my mother and whatever I have become today is because of her." Gunawati also possessed exceptional culinary skills. Though CK enjoyed all kinds of foods, be it Indian or continental, but he preferred the South Indian or Andhra style food cooked by his wife. Gunawati was not only good in managing the house, but she also had other talents. About her mother, Chandra Nayudu writes, "She certainly lived up to her name Gunawati (Gunawati means talented in Hindi). In fact she was so skilled that she could repair any breakdown in electrical gadgets, water taps, gas lamps, etc." She would also encourage her kids to take part in all extracurricular activities like music, sports and painting among others.

Cricket or sports was not the only topic of discussion among the family members. CK was a man who had a great knowledge on any subject and he could keep everyone engrossed for hours with his stories. Two of his daughters, Ahilya and Sunalini were good painters. And CK used to proudly show their paintings to the visitors. But the atmosphere at the house was one full of sporting activities. CK was of the belief that being involved in sporting activities helped in maintaining good health. So, there definitely was a lot of focus on sports. Table Tennis matches used to be organized at the house among the family members.

It was probably as a result of this stress on sports that many of his children and grandchildren represented their states and the nation in various sports. Both his sons played First-Class Cricket for Madhya Pradesh. His Son Prakash Nayudu was also a National Juniors Table Tennis Champion. CK's grandson and Prakash's son, Pratap Nayudu became an International Arm-Wrestling champion. I have already mentioned about his grandson Vijay Nayudu who represented Madhya Pradesh in the Ranji Trophy. It is worthwhile to remind that CK's brother, CS Nayudu also played test cricket for India. It is learnt that CK used to like his younger brother CS a lot and the two played together for a long time in the Holkar team. To have so many sportspersons from one family is rare and CK deserves the credit for this.

But one thing which CK's children missed as a result of his strictness was a visit to the theatres. In his book, Prakash Nayudu writes, "Going to the movies was strictly prohibited to us by Col. Nayudu. A taboo! Only when a religious or good social film would be screened then we would be allowed to go and view." The only time his children would watch a commercial movie was when he was out of town. So, despite being a man who travelled around the world, CK was orthodox in many ways. Though, it appears that he relaxed some of the norms in the latter part of his life. For instance, his daughter Chandra played the role of a chauffeur for most of the family needs. This was earlier an unthinkable act in the Nayudu household as girls were not allowed to go outside the house unescorted. But looking back, none of his children have any complaints about the restrictions imposed by CK. In fact, many of them consider that whatever they have achieved in life would not have been possible without the disciplined life that they led under CK.

Probably, the only vice that CK had was that he used to smoke a lot. Panama cigarette and Havana cigars were his favorite. Cricketer DB Deodhar, who lived till the age of 101 years, had attributed CK's relatively early death to his smoking. It is difficult to comment on the role played by smoking to his ill-health in the later stages, but his life had seen it all - professional success, a good family life and an unfortunate isolation in the last stages. But as CK had himself once said, "I have had my innings, it is for others to corner the glory now".

Number Game

Test Matches						
Batting						
Matches	***Innings***	***Runs***	***Average***	***Highest Score***	***100s***	***50s***
7	14	350	25.00	81	0	2
Bowling						
Matches	***Innings***	***Wickets***	***Average***	***Best Bowling***	***Econo-my***	***Strike Rate***
7	10	9	42.88	3-40	2.69	95.33

First-Class Matches						
Batting						
Matches	***Innings***	***Runs***	***Average***	***Highest Score***	***100s***	***50s***
207	344	11,825	35.94	200	26	58

Bowling					
Matches	***Wickets***	***Average***	***Best Bowling***	***5Ws in an Innings***	***10Ws in a Match***
207	411	29.28	7-44	12	2

Bombay Quadrangular & Pentangular Matches Batting							
Tournament	***Matches***	***Innings***	***Runs***	***Average***	***Highest Score***	***100s***	***50s***
Quadrangular	25	44	1934	48.35	155	5	12
Pentangular	5	8	222	31.71	66	-	1
Total	**30**	**52**	**2156**	**45.87**	**155**	**5**	**13**

List of centuries			
S.No	***Score***	***Opposition***	***Year***
1.	121	Parsees	1920
2.	135	Europeans	1924
3.	155	Muslims	1929
4.	129	Parsees	1935
5.	101	Muslims	1935

List of fifties			
S.No	***Score***	***Opposition***	***Year***
1.	80*	Parsees	1917
2.	56	Parsees	1919

3.	62	Muslims	1920
4.	51	Muslims	1920
5.	82	Muslims	1922
6.	76	Europeans	1923
7.	74	Europeans	1923
8.	52	Muslims	1924
9.	75	Parsees	1929
10.	97	Muslims	1934
11.	53	Muslims	1934
12.	53	Muslims	1935
13.	66	Muslims	1938

Bowling				
Tournament	***Matches***	***Wicket***	***Average***	***Best Bowling***
Quadrangular	25	29	31.24	3-26
Pentangular	5	9	31.11	3-87
Total	30	38	31.21	3-26

Highest Run Aggregates in the Bombay Tournament

S. No	***Player***	***Team***	***Matches***	***Innings***	***Runs***	***Average***	***Highest Score***	***100s***	***50s***
1.	CK Nayudu	Hindus	30	52	2156	45.87	155	5	13
2.	Vijay Merchant	Hindus	19	26	1965	109.16	250*	7	6
3.	JG Greig	Europeans	30	51	1785	39.16	184	2	11
4.	DB Deodhar	Hindus	31	53	1543	35.06	135	1	12
5.	P Vithal	Hindus	26	46	1290	30.71	108	2	6
6.	LP Jai	Hindus	25	41	1284	32.71	156	3	6
7.	S Wazir Ali	Muslims	19	33	1268	40.90	197	5	5
8.	VS Hazare Sr	The Rest	8	14	1212	101.00	309	4	4
9.	HJ Vajifdar	Parsees	28	49	1201	26.68	118	1	10
10.	KM Mistry	Parsees	30	54	1084	20.45	95	-	6

Ranji Trophy ***Batting***				
Innings	***Runs***	***Average***	***Highest Score***	***100s***
73	2567	36.67	200	5

List of centuries (all made playing for Holkars)			
S.No	***Score***	***Opposition***	***Year***
1.	102	Bengal	1942-43
2.	102	United Province	1943-44
3.	141	Bengal	1944-45
4.	101	Mysore	1945-46
5.	200	Baroda	1945-46

Cricketers with longest First-Class Career						
S.No	***Player***	***Country***	***Career Span***	***No. of Years***	***Year of Birth***	***Age during last match***
1.	CK Nayudu	India	1916-1963	47	1895	68
2.	WG Grace	England	1865-1908	43	1848	60
3.	AW Nourse	South Africa	1896-1935	39	1878	57
4.	GH Hirst	England	1891-1929	38	1871	58
5.	FA Tarrant	Australia	1898-1936	38	1880	55

My Inspiration and journey

When I began writing this book, many people had asked me why a book on Col. CK Nayudu now? Well, I wouldn't exaggerate and just for the sake of it say that CK was always my hero. The truth is that having written many articles on cricket, I wanted to take the next step and write a book about this glorious game we all love so much. So, I began researching on the topics or cricketers on whom I could write. Now, over the years Indian cricket has produced a pantheon of stars. This meant that there was not a shortage of topics to choose from.

I started looking at players from the time when Indian cricket began and that's when I came across the name 'Col CK Nayudu'. I had known that he was India's first test captain, but my knowledge about him was limited. As I explored more about him from the information available on the internet, his story seemed fascinating to me. At this stage, one thing that was clear to me was that he was for sure Indian cricket's first superstar. Further, it struck me that this year was his 50th death anniversary. Coincidentally, he passed away on November 14th, 1967, and 18 years later, I was born on the same day in 1985.

That's when I began wondering, that a book on him this year could be my humble tribute to the great man. The other thing was that, for me there couldn't have been a better way to start my career as an author than to write a book on Indian cricket's first superstar. The next step was to find out about people who could help me with stories about CK. This was a crucial task as very less information about him was available on the public domain. Thanks to my father, I got connected with CK's grandson Vijay Nayudu. Initially, he too was skeptical about my idea to have a book on his grandfather. But gradually, he agreed to help me out. I still remember the discussion which I had with him over phone when he seemed somewhat convinced about my proposal. Rightfully, he had said, I will provide you the right contacts, but you need to meet the people who actually played with CK or had at least seen him play. This turned out to be the best advice that he had given me.

With the list of ex-cricketers, administrators, CK's family members, I began my journey and it did turn out to be a memorable one. To be frank, I wasn't sure about how receptive these people would be to a first-time author like me. I was doubtful if I would even get an appointment with them. But as it turned out to be, I found that they were extremely kind and supportive in my endeavor. Most of them encouraged me and this gave me the confidence to proceed.

The first person whom I met during my research was former Indian cricketer Madhav Apte. Seated at his sea-facing penthouse in South Mumbai, we spoke for couple of hours about CK and cricket in general. And by the time I left his house, I was more than convinced that CK's story deserved to be told to the younger generation. The next person whom I met in this journey was 97 years old Vasant Raiji. Raiji is a cricket historian, who had written a book on CK years back and is one of CK's biggest fans. Even at this age, there was an excitement written all over his face as he spoke about CK. He admitted that he may not remember the finer details at this age, but I was stunned when many of the numbers that he mentioned about CK's career were completely accurate. I was short of words, when with the help of a walker, he came out to see me off till the lift. Similar to Raiji, I could sense the excitement in the voice of 90 years old MK Shukla, with whom I spoke to over the phone. Shukla had played alongside CK in the Holkar team. Unfortunately, I did not get the privilege of meeting MK Shukla and he passed away before my book could be published. I hope he is reading this book from up there in the Heavens

Afterwards, I met Vijay Nayudu, the man without whom this book would not have been possible. While, it was obvious for me to go to any of these meetings with proper preparation. But to my pleasant surprise, Vijay uncle was more prepared than me. Before I came, he had kept ready all the books, photos and documents related to his grandfather. We talked at length about CK and I must say that there was a unique humbleness in the way he spoke. He again emphasized that I needed to meet people who were from a generation earlier than him. I was asked to go to Indore, the 'Karmabhoomi' of CK to meet his former Holkar team-mates.

The Indore leg of my expedition began with a visit to the house of ex-Holkar player, Waman Jagtap. Such was his enthusiasm, that even at 87 years of age, he would get up in zest and demonstrate a shot to me. I was slowly understanding the respect that the Holkar players had for Colonel Saab. Post our discussion, he took me along on his scooter to a nearby restaurant for lunch. I was speechless at this hospitality and by the fact that he was still easily riding a scooter at this age. To me it seemed as though the people of Indore truly believed in "Atithi Devo Bhava (The guest is equivalent to God)". Whomsoever I met in Indore, welcomed me with a warmth which is slowly disappearing from our society. Be it the oldest surviving Holkar player, Rameshwar Pratap Singh, Akshay Dhakad (member of Madhya Pradesh Cricket Association whose father used to collect cricket books and paper cuttings), Prof. Suryaprakash Chaturvedi (who has written a book on CK in Hindi), Pratap Nayudu or Sanjay Jagdale; all welcomed me wholeheartedly. While this definitely is testimony to the goodwill of these people, but it also tells us about the amount of respect that they have for CK. Rameshwar Pratap Singh proudly showed me his photo along with the five-other centurions from the 1945-46 Ranji Trophy semi-final.

When I saw the collections of articles and books of Akshay Dhakad's father, I was like a child in a candy shop. There was so much information that he possessed. There were newspaper cuttings from the time India had played its first test match. Similarly, Prof. Chaturvedi whom I met at a Hindi Sahitya Samellan function had loads of stories to tell about CK. He even gifted me the book that he had written on CK.

A trip to Indore would have been incomplete without visiting the Holkar stadium. Thankfully for me, Sanjay Jagdale invited me to the Holkar stadium and showed me the belongings of CK. The likes of Sanjay Jagdale have guaranteed that the Holkar stadium breathes in an air of CK. The stadium is like a museum dedicated to CK, full of his photos and personal belongings. As I left Indore, I thanked God for making me meet such wonderful people who made me understand the oner named Col. CK Nayudu.

My next stop was in Pune at the residence of former Indian cricketer and administrator Chandu Borde. Being a cricketer and a selector himself, he gave me rare insights about CK Nayudu as a selector. He told me, "Throughout my career, Col. CK Nayudu was the most attractive player on the cricket field". This line coming from a cricketer who has seen and played with some of the all-time greats is an attestation of the manner in which CK played.

The road to unravel the greatness about CK, then took me to Jamnagar, the city of Ranjit Sinhji. Here, I met the heartthrob of yesteryears - Salim Durani. As said earlier, both Salim and his father had the distinction of playing first-class cricket with CK. And this for me, defined the word longevity with respect to CK. I was taken aback by the simplicity of Salim Durani, who leads a quiet life these days in Jamnagar. Much like he entertained the crowd with his sixes during his playing days, I found him to be a charmer with words. Encouraging me for my initiative to write a book on CK, he told me, "You are doing a great job. I wish you all the success". This statement ignited a new fire within me to work even harder for the book.

While the people from the cricketing community whom I met were pleased to know about my initiative. But some of CK's family members like his grandson Pratap Nayudu, whom I met in his office in Indore, went a step ahead and thanked me. This touched me a lot. Likewise, CK's daughter Leela Vidyasagar was extremely happy when she heard that a book is being written on her father. Leela's daughter Sangeeta who had helped me connect with her told me, "I am so happy to know that people haven't forgotten my nanaji".

In my reply to her, I will quote Bruce Lee who had said, "The key to immortality is first living a life worth remembering". And CK's life was more than worth remembering. I just hope that my humble writing has been able to do justice to the phenomenon named CK.

Author with
Salim Durani

Author with
Sanjay Jagdale

Author with Chandu Borde

Author with Waman Jagtap

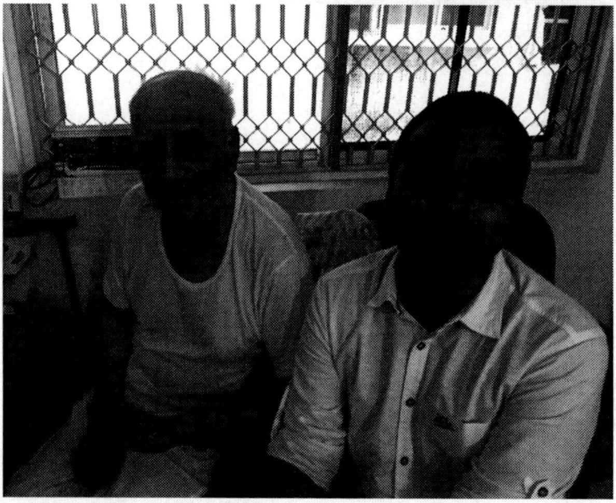

Author with Rameshwar Pratap Singh

Author with Vasant Raiji

Author with Madhav Apte

Other #SMBooks

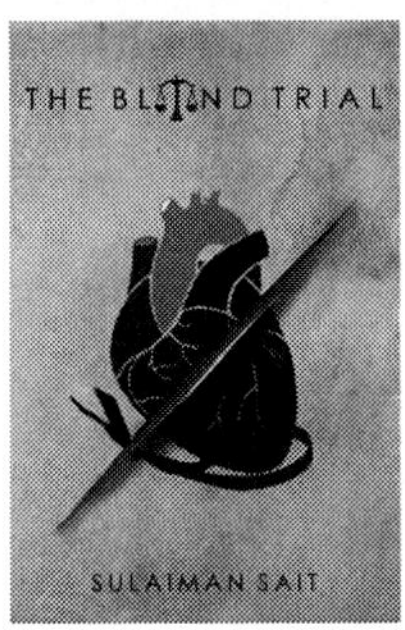

Other #SMBooks